Tris

Sams **Teach Yourself**

Foursquare

in **10 Minutes**

Indiana 46240

Sams Teach Yourself Foursquare in 10 Minutes

ISBN-13: 978-0-6723-3349-1

ISBN-10: 0-6723-3349-x

Library of Congress Cataloging-in-Publication data is on file.

First Printing: December 2010

Trademarks

All terms mentioned in this book that are known to be trademarks or service marks have been appropriately capitalized. Sams Publishing cannot attest to the accuracy of this information. Use of a term in this book should not be regarded as affecting the validity of any trademark or service mark.

Warning and Disclaimer

Every effort has been made to make this book as complete and as accurate as possible, but no warranty or fitness is implied. The information provided is on an "as is" basis. The author and the publisher shall have neither liability nor responsibility to any person or entity with respect to any loss or damages arising from the information contained in this book.

Bulk Sales

Sams Publishing offers excellent discounts on this book when ordered in quantity for bulk purchases or special sales. For more information, please contact

> U.S. Corporate and Government Sales
> 1-800-382-3419
> corpsales@pearsontechgroup.com

For sales outside the United States, please contact

> International Sales
> international@pearson.com

Associate Publisher
Greg Wiegand

Acquisitions Editor
Michelle Newcomb

Development Editor
Todd Brakke

Managing Editor
Sandra Schroeder

Project Editor
Seth Kerney

Copy Editor
Kitty Wilson

Indexer
Erika Millen

Proofreader
Apostrophe Editing Services

Technical Editor
Catherine Winters

Publishing Coordinator
Cindy Teeters

Book Designer
Gary Adair

Compositor
Trina Wurst

Contents

About the Author

This is the third book from **Tris Hussey**, a long-time technologist, blogger, and writer. Tris started blogging on a whim in 2004 and quickly became Canada's first professional blogger and a leading expert in business blogging. He has been a part of several Web 2.0 startups, from blogging software to blogging agencies.

In addition to writing and consulting, Tris gives workshops and teaches classes on social media, blogging, podcasting, and WordPress at the University of British Columbia and the British Columbia Institute of Technology. Tris contributes to many online news and technology sites. His home base online is trishussey.com.

Tris lives and works in beautiful Vancouver, British Columbia.

Dedication

For my children, Aislinn and Tenzin. You are by far my greatest creation and legacy in this world.

Acknowledgments

No author completes a book alone. I have many, many people to thank for helping me complete this book. Thanks to my wife, Sheila, who puts up with my author's temperament with such grace. Thanks also to my editor, Michelle, whose steadfast support and suggestions for new books keeps me happily busy. Finally, thank you to my technical editor, Catherine, who had to trudge through some dreadful early chapters to get us to this point. I thank you all.

Introduction

How to describe Foursquare? Just calling it a location-based game would be too simplistic—even though that's how it was originally billed. It's a little frightening to call it a great way to find, track down, and stalk your friends. Foursquare is, simply, a way to let friends know what places you like, go to often, and identify with. Foursquare is a service in the ever-growing ecosystem of social media tools where you have friends and followers, and you're sharing something about yourself with them. In Foursquare's case, you're sharing where you are. This book provides all the information you need to start using Foursquare quickly and, most of all, *safely*. With Foursquare you are, after all, telling people where you are. It's therefore important to use it safely.

Safety lectures aside, I get a lot of fun out of using Foursquare to learn about places my friends visit. ("Hey! You're right around the corner! How about if I swing by…?"). And I like vying for more points in the game and trying to oust friends as "mayors" of our favorite haunts. Foursquare is an evolution of how we are sharing more and more information through social media. It used to be sharing things through Facebook was enough, then we added Twitter to the mix, and now Foursquare gives us a way to let our friends know about our favorite coffee place, brunch place, and shop for the coolest new geek toys.

About This Book

Like all other *Sams Teach Yourself in 10 Minutes* books, this book is broken up into sections that you can read and work through in 10 minutes each. Each one presents straightforward tasks or ideas that have real outcomes. Throughout the book, you will at times need to venture away from your computer, but don't worry: You'll be well prepared when you get going.

Who This Book Is For

This book is for those with a bit of wanderlust mixed with an interest in social media. Foursquare isn't hard or even complicated to use. You go out and about anyway, and using Foursquare can just make it that much more fun.

What You Need as You Use This Book

Beyond a willingness to learn and a bit of a sense of adventure, you're going to need a computer with an Internet connection *and* a mobile phone (or another mobile wireless device). This is the key part of Foursquare: While you can create your account and manage friends on the website, you need a mobile device to "check in" at locations.

You can use Foursquare on BlackBerry phones, iPhones, iPod Touches, iPads, Windows Mobile devices, and Android-based devices. If you're using a "regular" mobile phone (not a smartphone) in the United States, you can check in by sending a text. Mobile devices can all coordinate using GPS or the cellular network, so your actual location can be confirmed. (No cheating, people!)

Conventions Used in This Book

Like all other *Sams Teach Yourself* books, this one contains more than just the text. Elements such as the following draw your attention to additional information throughout the book:

> TIP
> Tips offer helpful shortcuts or easier ways to do something.

> **NOTE**
>
> Notes are extra bits of information related to the text that might help you expand your knowledge or understanding of what I'm talking about.

> **CAUTION**
>
> Cautions are warnings or other important information you need to know about consequences of using a feature or executing a task.

> **PLAIN ENGLISH**
>
> Plain English sidebars provide clear definitions of new essential terms.

A Note About Screenshots and Examples

The Internet and social media are funny things. These things change so quickly that a site or mobile application might look very different one day than it looked the day before. Therefore, keep in mind that the sites you pull up today may not look *exactly* like the ones shown in this book's screenshots. In addition, different sites have different looks in different web browsers. Most of the screenshots of the Foursquare website in this book were taken with either the Google Chrome or Apple Safari web browsers. Your results may vary.

This book uses the most recent screenshots available. I'm posting major updates at this book's site, at teachyourselffoursquare.com.

What Is Foursquare?

In this lesson we cover the basics of what Foursquare is all about, and how it works, using geolocation and geotagging to place you on a map.

How Foursquare Works

At its heart, Foursquare is a locationally aware game—a game based on doing things related to where you are in the world. The core of Foursquare is to "check in" at the places you frequent (stores, restaurants, events, anything that has a location) and, as you check in, you earn points. As you earn points and check in, you earn badges. The badges can be silly, like the Player badge when you happen to check into a location with lots of members of the opposite sex. Or they can be tied to an event, like the Swarm badge, when 50 or more people check into a location within a short period of time.

As at all other social media sites, at Foursquare.com you have friends and followers (see Figure 1.1). Your *friends* are people who you allow to know where you are; *followers* are those who allow you to know where they are. While it's fun to follow lots of people in your own city, it's also fun to follow people you know *outside* where you live. One of the aspects of Foursquare is letting people know about locations in the area. For example, say that you check into a coffee shop, and you get a note about the shop: A friend said (at some point in the past) that, if you're hungry, Tony's Tuna Tikihut (a different store, but near where you are now) has the best sandwiches, and the super-duper tuna melt is the one to order. Since a person you ostensibly know and trust has given this recommendation, you might be inclined to act on it.

Where Do These Notes and Tips Come From?

Tips and notes come from a couple places. First you can add a tip or note when you check-in (more in Lesson 4, "Mobile Application"), and you see the tips and notes your friends have already entered. You can also add tips and notes to a venue on the website. Tips and notes are probably the most valuable part of Foursquare!

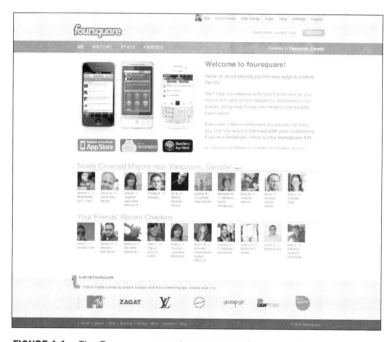

FIGURE 1.1   The Foursquare.com home page (after you log in).

PLAIN ENGLISH: **Social Media**

Social media (or *social networking*, if you prefer) is a catch-all term that applies to sites such as Twitter, Facebook, Foursquare, MySpace, LinkedIn, and blogs. These sites and services are based on connecting people into larger, Internet-based social networks.

Social media has become a buzzword that some people feel gives the sites near-magical powers. In reality, it just means that they help us use the Internet to connect to each other more easily.

Understanding the Basic Idea

As mentioned earlier, the basic idea of Foursquare is that you "check into" places you visit. Stop for a coffee; check in. Pick up some groceries; check in. Museum, party, conference, you name it—if you can locate it, you can check into it. Part of Foursquare is a game where each check-in earns you points. You get a certain number of points for your first check-in of the day, bonus points if it's your first time there, and so on. You get even more points if you add a new location to Foursquare, but I'll talk more about that in Lesson 5, "Checking In."

As you check in more places, a few things happen beyond the whole points thing. One is that you earn *badges*. Some badges are funny, like I'm on a Boat! if you are, well, on a boat. The other thing that can happen is that if you check into a place more than any other person over a period of time, you can become "mayor" of that location. Sure, it's easy to be mayor of your house, but mayor of a busy place like a coffee shop might take more doing. Initially, being mayor of a place didn't get you anything, but now, as more and more people are using Foursquare, businesses have figured out that rewarding mayors with discounts or freebies is a fantastic way to reward loyal customers and keep people coming back. Again, more on that later.

Another part of Foursquare's social media-powered, game is that you can see where your friends are at any given time. Maybe you're hungry and looking for a place to grab a snack, so you check Foursquare to see if (a) any of your friends are in the area or (b) if they have *recommended* something in the area with Tips and Recommendations.

How Foursquare Started

Foursquare founders Dennis Crowley and Naveen Selvadurai met in 2007 in New York City. They were sharing office space, though working for different companies at the time. As a lot of these ideas happen, I can imagine how Foursquare came about:

> "Hey wouldn't it be great if there were a way that we could see where all our friends were hanging out around the city?"

"Yeah, and what if we made it a game, too, see who could earn the most points in a week?"

"Right, and we could also let our friends give us tips about places to go, things to do, that kind of stuff."

That, pretty much, is what Foursquare became. Talking with Erin Gleason, who is responsible for PR at Foursquare, she confirmed my gut feeling about the intention of the game: "See where your friends are, find new places to go to, encourage friendly competition with a game."

There are some really interesting facts about how Foursquare started. First, originally it was available only in a few select U.S. cites and Amsterdam, in the Netherlands. Next, only "superuser" level users could add or edit venues. You didn't achieve superuser level until you had a large number of check-ins and held some mayorships. But that all changed September 9, 2009. That was the day Foursquare opened up in Vancouver, British Columbia, and everything about Foursquare changed overnight.

When Foursquare came to Canada, at the behest and prodding of Chris Breikss of 6S Marketing, there was a problem. How was Foursquare going to prepopulate enough venues? In reality, it couldn't, so what it did instead was allow everyone to add venues. Foursquare switched to a "crowdsourced" model of expanding: Foursquare users became responsible for the growth of Foursquare, and the result was amazing.

In short order, and in plenty of time for the official launch party (yes, I was there), hundreds of venues were added in Vancouver. Montreal and Toronto were the next two Canadian cities added to the list, and both launches were equally successful. If you're wondering, yeah....These three launches were *essential* to how Foursquare has grown. Once people could register, mark their home town as any city, and add venues themselves, Foursquare was able to grow on its own. It could grow and grow into any corner of the world.

> PLAIN ENGLISH: **Crowdsourcing**
>
> *Crowdsourcing* is based on the idea of letting users (or "the crowd") help you with a particular task, such as adding new venues to Foursquare. Instead of hiring people to do the work, you crowdsource it—sort of like outsourcing. It has become pretty common within the social media world for companies to let the users of a service help expand and fill it with information. This leads to (a) users feeling like they own a piece of the site's success and (b) saving a small fortune in startup money by not having to pay for the work!

When I paid a visit to B.C.'s Okanagan Valley (home of some of the best vineyards in the world), I was able to check into a small winery on Foursquare. I had wanted to be the person to add the new venue but was actually pleasantly surprised that the winery was already there!

It's important to understand that the essence of Foursquare hasn't changed: It's still about checking in, seeing where friends are, and learning about new places. But once Foursquare opened up to the whole world, the "game" changed. I think it changed the game for the better. Much better.

Location: Social Games

Remember I said that Foursquare is a game? Honestly, I don't know many people who use it *as* a game (and Vancouver is a pretty Foursquare-savvy city), but there is that points thing that you see as you check into places. Does it matter? Should you care? I don't think so. I use Foursquare, as do most of my friends, as a way to let each other know where we are and to share information about the places we like to go. Sure, the badges are fun (like the Jobs badge if you check into an Apple Store three times), but they are more like bling than something to worry about.

> NOTE
>
> The people at Foursquare are already looking at how to revitalize and revamp the game aspect of Foursquare. The rules of the game and how it works haven't changed since Foursquare launched in 2009, but since then *how* people use Foursquare *has changed* tremendously. So don't be surprised if by the time this book is in your hands, there are many new aspects of the "game" part of Foursquare.

That said, you do earn points for each check-in, more points if it's your first time there, and yet more points if it's a new venue. You even get bonus points for checking into lots of places in one day/night. I think that while Foursquare *started* out as a game, it's evolving into something entirely different. Where it's going we can't be too sure—remember that Foursquare is just a little over a year old—but having easy tools to change the places we like to visit is something that *a lot* of people love to do.

Before I get into what those tools are all about, you need to understand geotagging and geolocation.

Geotagging and Geolocation

Two essential concepts that make Foursquare work are geotagging and geolocation. Geotagging is simply connecting places with pictures or other information on the Internet, such as reviews or websites. It works like this: Your smart phone uses GPS to "know" where it is. You take a picture of a statue, and you can have your phone geotag that picture with where it actually is. You can then gather all your pictures together by place and, if you upload the pictures to the Internet, that geolocation information is saved as well, so other people can find your picture when searching for pictures taken in that general area. Geolocation is simply just locating something on a map and connecting it together on the Internet.

Foursquare puts together the pieces of where you are (such as in a store) with other information, such as what else is close by, how often you've been there, and maybe suggestions and tips from other users. You couldn't, for example, know that just around the corner is the best sushi place in the city if someone hadn't checked in there in Foursquare and added that additional geotagged information that it was great.

PLAIN ENGLISH: **Geotagging and Geolocation**

Geolocation means that a device (like a smartphone) or application (like Foursquare) knows where you are in the world so that information can be used to help you. *Geotagging* means taking that geolocated information and *adding* it to something like a picture as part of its information (meta data), such as when it was taken and what kind of camera took the picture. Foursquare works because nearly every mobile device you own knows where you are already.

At first this might seem confusing, but as you're using Foursquare, you don't have to think about geotagging and geolocation; it just happens as you use Foursquare. Foursquare is part of the larger world of geolocation and geotagging. It's very much like how, on Google Maps, you can see what types of restaurants, attractions, or places are around an address you enter. Google already gathers information (pictures, business listings, websites) that has geographic information tied to it (like the address of a museum), so Google can easily just overlay that information into things like Google Maps and other Google searches. Welcome to the new world of information.

Why Use Foursquare?

Why bother with Foursquare? Well, it's fun. When you're at a big get-together with a bunch of friends, it's fun to check in and see how many of your other friends are there, too. And it's fun to get a tip on the best thing to order at a restaurant from a friend who has been there before. Foursquare offers fun, easy ways to use technology that can help you learn about what your friends like. And as more businesses offer deals to frequent customers through Foursquare check-ins, you'll be able to save you money, too!

Sure, I test and use a lot of the new social media tools that come out. I try to test all of them as they come out, actually. I think there's something unique about Foursquare. Yes, it's still early days, and I think the most interesting things are yet to come, but I think using something that is fun *and* has the potential for a lot more in the future is pretty exciting.

Summary

Foursquare is a social media game in which you check into the places you visit day-to-day. Checking in earns you points and badges. And if you check into a place often, you can become mayor of that place. It all starts at Foursquare.com, but you predominantly use Foursquare through mobile devices such as cell phones.

LESSON 2

Creating a Foursquare Account

In this lesson we'll go through the (simple) process of setting up your Foursquare account including filling out your profile and how to find friends on Foursquare.

Joining Foursquare

Now that you have a handle on what Foursquare is all about, it's time to get into the game and create your account. Basically, Foursquare needs to know who you are and where you are (as a home base). This lesson starts off by having you head to Foursquare.com and look for the big Join Now button.

Getting started with Foursquare is easy and takes just a couple minutes. After you click the Join Now button, you see a simple web form. You just fill in the required fields (the ones with * next to them) and click Join to start the ball rolling (see Figure 2.1).

Although the signup process at Foursquare isn't anything special or unique, there are some considerations that you should think about before just clicking Join. In today's world, we need to always be mindful of our personal privacy and security.

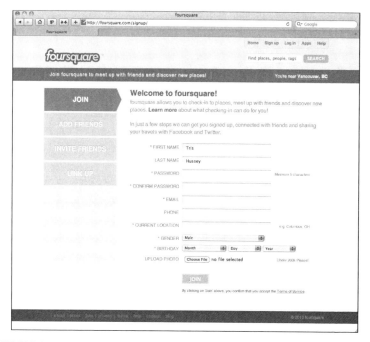

FIGURE 2.1   The signup form for to create a Foursquare account.

TIP

Picking good passwords doesn't mean using your dog's birthday; it means being subtle and clever. One of the tricks to great passwords is thinking in terms of *phrases* instead of *words*. Most people use maybe one or two words for their password. These days, this just doesn't cut it. Try something different. Take a phrase like "I drink orange pekoe tea" and switch out letters for numbers and symbols so you get something like this: 1dr1nkOr@ng3p3kO3t3@!. (I included the ! here just to give the password a little oomph.) This works by swapping "i" with 1, "o" with a zero, "e" with 3 and "a" with @, the longer the phrase the better, but even a short phrase of two or three words is good. How strong is this as a password? According to HowSecureIsMyPassword.net, it would take 988 *quintillion* years (a quintillion is a 1 with 18 zeros behind it) for an ordinary desktop PC to crack that password. Think you can remember that one?

Who Are You?

From a privacy standpoint, I know a lot of people are a bit skittish about giving out personal information on sites like Foursquare. You should be. I am, too. For example, when I *must* put in my birthday, I put in something *close* to my real birthday. Close enough so that my age is right, but not so close that it could be used for identity theft.

Taking that step is simple enough, but what about something like whether to enter your last name? Although this treads into dangerous privacy waters, I encourage you to put your last name into the Foursquare field. Why? It makes it easier for your friends to find you *and* to confirm you as a friend. Foursquare is one of the few social media sites where I'm a little more picky than others when choosing whom to add as friend. The whole locational aspect, I think, should have most people think for a moment before accepting any and all friend requests. I'll talk more about privacy throughout this book, but for now, just consider that if you use your real last name *and* use a picture of yourself that your friends recognize, your chances of them accepting your friendship request are much better.

Speaking of pictures, those little pictures (they're called *avatars*) are key to social network profiles. Yes, they are just like Facebook profile photos, but they are usually square and smaller than what you see on Facebook. I try to make sure I have a good picture that looks like me for all my services. No cute little icons or cartoons, just me. Like putting in your last name, using a real (and decent) picture of yourself helps make sure your friends know it's you. That said, putting a real picture of me on my profile is my own choice, and if you want to use some other icon, that's just fine, too.

Where Are You?

While it's only one wee little box, setting your current location is important to Foursquare. It gives you a "home base" when you are starting to add friends and before you start checking into places. Foursquare updates your location as you check in on your mobile client, but to start out, it needs to know where you actually are. This not only gives you a starting point, but also when you start adding friends, potential friends can match a name, a face, *and* a place to know they are adding the person they think they are. ("Oh *that* Jill, the one from Georgia....")

Adding Friends

After you've given Foursquare info about yourself, the next step is to add your first batch of friends. The easiest way to do this is to connect with either Twitter or Facebook to see which of your friends there are already using Foursquare (see Figure 2.2). Which service to start with is your choice. I chose Twitter when I started off because that's where I have connected with more friends (I'm a well-known Facebook curmudgeon), but if most of your friends are on Facebook, use that one.

> **NOTE**
>
> You don't have to use either Facebook or Twitter to use Foursquare, they just make it easier to find people you know. You can always look for people by name or email address. In Lesson 3, "Friends," I talk about how to use your address book to find and add friends.

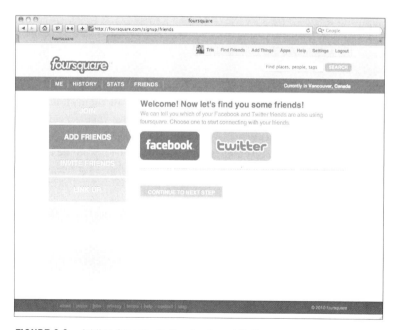

FIGURE 2.2   Adding friends via Facebook and Twitter.

With either service, you need to authorize Foursquare to access your account on the other service. For both Facebook and Twitter you see a pop-up window that asks if you want to make the connection. Click Connect for Facebook or Allow for Twitter, and you see a list of potential friends to start connecting with. You don't have to go hog wild here and add everyone at once. You can start with a small set and add more friends later. Click Continue to the Next Step when you're done. I'll talk more about friends in the next lesson.

Inviting Friends

Didn't see your best buds as existing Foursquare users? No problem. You can invite them to join Foursquare. Initially, you can use Facebook and Twitter to invite friends, but you can also invite them by email. Here is one place where my advice might clash with conventional wisdom: I say that unless you don't have *anyone* you know already using Foursquare, I wouldn't invite people right now. Although it seems counterintuitive, I think inviting someone completely new to a new service that you're just learning too doesn't help either of you very much. Chances are that *someone* you know on Facebook or Twitter is also on Foursquare. Start with these folks. Not only can they help you learn the ropes, they also can connect you with lots of other Foursquare users, too. (The irony is that in many cases, I don't follow this advice when I join a new service, but I have a good reason: I'm often trying out brand-new services, and I need to invite people who would also be interested in trying it to help figure it out.)

> TIP
>
> When you're trying out these new services, the people to add are the trusty geeks you know who might already be using it. They are the ones who can show you the ropes and all the inside tricks.

Once you add people, just click the Continue button for the next step. If you want to invite people by email, you just need their email address to invite them.

I'll talk more about friends in other lessons, especially Lesson 3, "Creating an Account."

Connecting to Other Social Media Sites

In social media, people like to hook together the various sites they use. If you chose to use Facebook or Twitter to find friends, those services are connected already. To double-check whether you've connected those services with Foursquare already, click Settings at the top of your screen—while you're logged in, of course—and scroll to the bottom of the resulting page. As in Figure 2.3, you see big Twitter and Facebook logos. If you click the logo for either service, Foursquare prompts you to allow that service to connect, so you can not only find friends but also post your updates there as well.

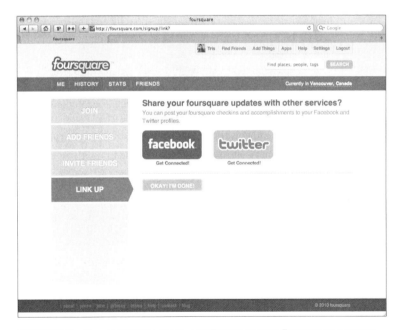

FIGURE 2.3   Connecting Facebook and Twitter to your Foursquare account.

The default setting for connecting services is that you send updates to those services when you check in (Lesson 5, "Checking In"), become mayor (Lesson 7, "Becoming a Mayor"), or unlock a badge (Lesson 6, "Badges"). As shown in Figure 2.4, I suggest *unchecking* sending all your check-ins to Facebook and Twitter.

FIGURE 2.4   Consider disabling the I Check-In setting for your linked accounts.

But this is a social site, so why wouldn't you want to tweet about your check-ins? Because it gets *really, really* annoying to send a constant stream of tweets or Facebook updates with your Foursquare check-ins. Yes, I know you'll see people doing it, but I suggest saving broadcasting where you are for special things like big events, conferences, and the like. These are times when a lot of people are checking in there, too. I occasionally send check-ins to Twitter for really cool or special places, but I don't do it often. I do let Foursquare update Twitter and Facebook when I earn a badge or become a mayor of a location because (a) they happen more rarely and (b) those are more interesting (I think). Your friends and followers might disagree with my advice, though, so if you want to tell the world, be my guest.

> **CAUTION**
>
> Here's another privacy warning: If you broadcast to Twitter and Facebook that you've just checked into a place, you've just told a whole bunch of people that you're not at home. You might trust your Foursquare friends, but do you trust your entire Facebook friend cadre and all your Twitter followers?

Deleting Your Account

If you decide Foursquare isn't for you, you can delete your account easily: Simply click the Delete Account link just below your Account Info block on your Settings page (refer to Figure 2.4). Foursquare asks for confirmation, but once you click that link, your Foursquare info is gone. If you change your mind and want to get back into Foursquare, you have to create another account, add friends again, earn badges, and become mayor all over again.

But why would you ever want to delete your account?

Summary

It took you no time at all to create an account on Foursquare! You'll be checking into your first locations soon. But this lesson got you only as far as setting up your account and requesting your first batch of friendships. The next lesson goes into a lot more detail about managing friends.

Friends

In this lesson you'll learn all about finding, adding, and managing friends. This isn't just about finding people to connect with either, because you must always keep your privacy, safety, and security in mind as well.

Resources for Locating Friends

As you might have gathered from Lesson 2, the folks at Foursquare know that you won't get a lot out of the service unless you have friends to share it with—so they encourage you to start adding friends right away. It's a good plan, but let's say you skipped that step or you want to add more friends later. How can you add friends to your network? There are a few basic ways to pull it off:

▶ Adding from Facebook

▶ Adding from Twitter

▶ Adding from Gmail contacts

▶ Inviting by email

▶ Adding friends of friends

▶ Searching Foursquare

You can use some of these methods from both the Foursquare website *and* mobile clients. Where you can't use a method on your smart phone, I note that it's *web only*.

> **NOTE**
>
> In the screenshots in this lesson, you might notice right away that there aren't any *people* in them. Well, the reason for this is that I respect my friends' privacy. To show the several hundred people from Twitter, Facebook, or Gmail whom I *could* add isn't fair to them. I do show a couple shots with real people, but I've used them with permission.

Finding Friends

Let's start with the three easiest ways to find friends via the Foursquare website (*web only*):

- ▶ Twitter

- ▶ Facebook

- ▶ Gmail

For each of these services, the process is (essentially) the same. You click the icon for the service, enter information, and then get a list of people to add (see Figure 3.1). You get to this key page by clicking Find Friends in the top menu bar next to your picture. (You did set up your avatar right?)

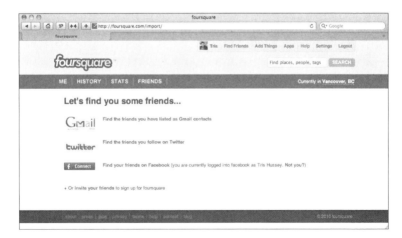

FIGURE 3.1 Finding Foursquare friends through Twitter, Facebook, and Gmail.

In the case of Gmail, you have to authorize Foursquare to access your address book on Gmail. When you select Gmail, you should see a screen like the one shown in Figure 3.2, prompting you to confirm which account to connect to. (You can see I have multiple email accounts.)

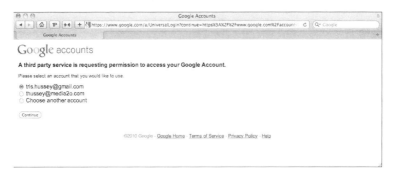

FIGURE 3.2   Giving Foursquare permission to access your Gmail account.

Foursquare tries to load the avatars from the various services, if it can. If someone doesn't have an avatar set for that service, or the other site is especially busy, the avatars might not be available to load. Having avatars at this point is like including locations and last names in your profile: Those pictures can be helpful in helping you pick out people you know.

Finding Friends of Friends

We've already looked at the easiest ways to add friends in Foursquare. But what about the "nearly as easy" ways to do it? Let's start with inviting friends of friends. This method is pretty simple:

1. Click the big Friends button on the navigation bar. Foursquare brings you to your Manage Friends screen (see Figure 3.3).

2. Click the Friends link.

3. Click any of your friends to see who they're friends with.

FIGURE 3.3 My Manage Friends screen (sorry not showing my friends for their privacy).

Here's the challenge on the web: You can't actually see a *list* of your friend's friends, just a few of the avatars (and small ones at that). If you recognize someone from that list, you can click his or her picture and see if you're already following the person. If not, you can add the person.

In contrast, on the mobile clients, you can see a list of the friends your friend is following and then click to see if you are following them.

> **NOTE**
>
> I find the differences between the mobile and web versions of Foursquare maddening sometimes. Having a simple list of users on the web version would be great. However, because Foursquare is very much a toddler in the world of social media, I think we can cut it some slack. For now.

Finding Friends via Your Mobile Phone

Can you find friends on your cell phone and on the web? Yes, you certainly can, in a couple different ways. I'll delve into how these functions work in Lesson 4. For now I'll say that you can find friends on the go through your address book, in Twitter, in Facebook, by name, or by phone number (see Figure 3.4). However, I think I'd be more likely to add friends through the check-in timeline on the mobile app because it's a lot easier and more straightforward than the other mobile options.

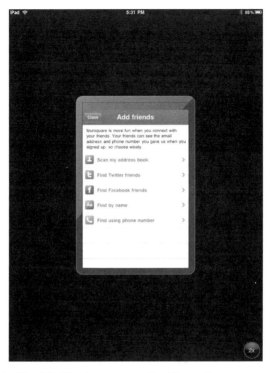

FIGURE 3.4   The Add Friends screen on the iPhone Foursquare app.

Adding Friends

As on Facebook, when you want to add someone as a friend on
Foursquare, the connection has to be mutual and reciprocal. You *request*
to follow/friend someone on Foursquare, and he or she has to accept the
request. It's not hard to see the logic in this. When you check into
Foursquare, you're telling the world where you are. This might not be
something you want to let just anyone know (hence the warnings in
Lesson 2 about Twitter and Facebook).

Remember, when you broadcast where you are (or not) through Twitter, it is *completely public*. Anyone can see that information. On Facebook the check-in is on your wall for all your Facebook friends to see (and friends of friends if a friend comments on your check-in). There are a lot of good reasons why you might be okay with telling the world where you are; however, there are just as many (maybe more) why you would not want to broadcast your location. Again, my personal choice is to *very rarely* broadcast my location to Facebook and/or Twitter. I am much more selective about choosing my Foursquare friends than I am with any other service. By the end of the book I might sound like a broken record about this topic, but I would be remiss if I didn't keep driving that point home.

As you might have figured out by now, the whole process of *finding* friends is really about *adding* friends. As you find friends via Twitter, Facebook, or Gmail, if there is someone you're not already friends with, you see a nice Add button (in a lovely shade of green) below the person's picture. When you click this button, Foursquare sends a request to that person, stating that you want to be friends him or her.

> NOTE
>
> You might happen upon some celebrities on Foursquare. (No, I don't count.) In these cases you'll notice that, although you can't *add* them, you can *follow* them instead. So, what's the difference? Celebrities love social media just like the rest of us, but the thing is that they want their *real* friends to be friends with them and just let the unwashed masses (that would be you and me)...well...get a different data stream. Therefore, they allow you to follow them rather than friend them. How do the real friends of celebs add them? Frankly I don't know. Foursquare keeps that info close to its vest.
>
> Brands are a different matter, as we discuss in Lesson 9, "Privacy and Safety."

You can see how many people you're waiting to hear from under Manage Friends and the Waiting to Hear From link. Don't take it personally if it takes a while to get a response from some people. Foursquare is just starting to catch on, and I don't think people have it in their daily social media routine to manage friend requests on Foursquare. (I tend to work through them about once a week.) Also don't take it personally if some people *never* accept your request (or ignore it). There's a really good reason for that: privacy and security.

Friending Etiquette in Social Media

There are times in this world when technology moves faster than does society's rules of etiquette. When the telephone was invented there were debates about what to say when you answer the phone. (Alexander Graham Bell advocated for "ahoy!") When email became popular there were debates about how to write emails and for what uses email was appropriate. With social media, we now have this whole system of "friends," and we haven't caught up with how to manage those relationships yet.

One of the places where things are far from worked out is what if someone doesn't friend you back on one service or another. Is it okay to ask people again? Should you send another request or just let it go? In the world of Foursquare I recommend just letting it go. If it comes up where they ask why you didn't know they were there or something, it's okay to say something like, "I don't think we're friends on Foursquare yet."

Remember, Foursquare deals with some pretty personal information. I don't accept all Foursquare friendship requests, and I recommend that you don't either.

In the mobile world (and again, I'll talk about this in more detail in the next lesson), when you're using Foursquare on the go, you can request to add people as friends as well. After your initial push, this is how you're most likely to add new friends. Say that you're at an event, a restaurant, or another locale, and you notice that there are other people checked in there. (You can see this when you're checking into a place by scrolling down in the check-in window.) You recognize one of the names, and you select them from the list. If the person isn't already a friend of yours, you see the Add <Name> as a Friend button on the screen. For example, Figure 3.5 shows the Add Beth as a Friend button.

By clicking this button, you can send off a friend request. As more and more people use Foursquare, I think this will become the most common way that people add new friends.

FIGURE 3.5   Adding a person as a friend through a mobile app (in this case on an iPhone).

Accepting Friend Requests

Once you start using Foursquare, people will likely want to be friends with you. You know that they found you using the same process you went through to find people to add. What you don't necessarily know is why they want to be friends with you. It comes back to that old devil privacy.

Every time a new friend request comes in, and especially if I don't recognize the person right off, I ask myself "Why me? Do I know this person? How might this person know me? Is this a friend of a friend? Or has this person seen my name in some social media article?" (It happens. I write books and speak at a lot of conferences.) Before I accept a friend, I make sure that I understand *why* the person might be asking in the first place. As you can gather, I don't accept friend requests from everyone. Unlike some other social media sites/services, I believe Foursquare requires a certain amount of *trust*. While I know many people I trust, even if I haven't met them in person, I don't trust everyone.

The mechanics of accepting a friend request are simple. Either from your Dashboard, as in Figure 3.6, or by clicking the Friends button on your cell phone, as in Figure 3.7, you just click Accept to accept or Ignore to, well, you know.

FIGURE 3.6 My Foursquare Dashboard, with the pending friend requests on the right.

FIGURE 3.7 On the Manage Friends screen, my pending friend requests.

So, with Foursquare, you find friends, you request them, and either they accept you or they ignore you. Hmm, kinda like middle school....

Summary

Finding and adding friends on Foursquare is pretty easy. The simplest way is to tap into the social networks you're already using (like Twitter and Facebook) or use your Gmail address book to find even more people. You'll probably start gathering more friends as you go, often when you begin to see familiar faces checking into places. But don't ever forget that when you let people into your Foursquare world, they can tell where you are—and where you're not. Exercising a bit of caution here is highly recommended.

LESSON 4

Mobile Applications

In this lesson we talk about how you're going to use Foursquare most of the time—your mobile device. I cover the official apps and mobile website here. The apps that other people have created can have varying degrees of quality, so they are something you should use at your own risk.

Getting the Right App for Your Device

Now that you have your Foursquare account and a few friends, it's time to start using Foursquare for real. If there's one thing that I find odd about Foursquare it's that Foursquare is the only social media tool/service that I know of where you can do *less* on the website through your computer than you can do on your mobile device. At first, this really, really didn't make sense to me. Why *can't* I check in on the website? I'm in my local coffee place, I'm already mayor here (more about this in Lesson 5), what's the deal?!

The deal is that while Foursquare *could* use the Google Maps API to have its main site find out where you are, it doesn't want to go in that direction right now. The game is about being out and about, not checking in with your laptop.

> NOTE
>
> "Wait, my iPad and iPod Touch knows where I am! I use Google Maps all the time with these devices that have only Wi-Fi!" Yes, I know. Those devices, and the iOS apps they run, are designed to tap into the location services in a device so that it knows where it is. Through the same process, you can check into locations with your laptop and the mobile website. Foursquare doesn't encourage people to do this because it can be used to cheat and game the system. However, yes, technically, you can check in using your laptop and the mobile website URL.

PLAIN ENGLISH: **API**

API stands for *application programming interface*. When people create new sites such as Foursquare, Twitter, and even Facebook, the developers of the sites provide a way for programmers to build upon what the sites have already built. This is done by providing a set of programming rules and tools that connect to the site and dictate how it works. With these tools, other programmers can build on and expand what the site originally developed and create new programs and services from them. These rules are called the API.

Essentially, a lot of what we use online today is built on pulling together the APIs, or sets of programming codes, from a variety of services and tools. The Connect to Facebook and Connect to Twitter buttons you saw when setting up your account work because they use the APIs from those services.

So, if you can't check in at the main website, what's it good for? The website is really the hub of it all. Although you can't use it to check in, you can use it for a number of tasks:

- ▶ Adding a tip about a venue or location

- ▶ Adding a new location

- ▶ Managing your friends

- ▶ Reviewing your check-in history

- ▶ Checking out your check-in statistics

- ▶ Editing venues

- ▶ Connecting your account to Twitter or Facebook

For the most important part of Foursquare, checking in, you need to have some kind of mobile, Internet-capable device (smart phone, cell phone, tablet, and so on). Like Twitter, Foursquare is, at its heart, a *mobile* application. It's a tool you use on the go (or going). Foursquare has done a great job of covering the major smart phones (iOS, Android, and BlackBerry devices) with native applications; you can also use Foursquare on any other devices that can get on the Internet with a mobile browser. For users in the United States, you can also use SMS short codes to check in. So, although the main website seems like a little "meh, so what," it's still important to know how the system works.

PLAIN ENGLISH: **SMS**

SMS stands for Short Message Service and is *essentially* synonymous with sending a text message on your cell phone. Technically there are other ways to send a text message from your phone, but SMS is the most common, and it's what most carriers use today.

Official Foursquare Apps

Foursquare has developed its own official applications for key mobile devices: iPhones, BlackBerry smart phones, and Android-based devices. These were some of the first apps that came out for Foursquare (beyond the mobile version of the website itself).

Although you can download Foursquare for your device from its app store, an even easier way is to visit m.foursquare.com on your device and follow the link to download the version of the app for your device. The link should point you to not only the correct store, but also the correct app. There are more and more apps that connect to Foursquare, but there are only a few official apps. It's also important to note that the official Foursquare apps are all free.

All the Foursquare mobile apps work, essentially, in the same way. While there might be a feature one has that another doesn't (for example, the iPhone and Android versions have a map to see where your friends are, but currently the BlackBerry version doesn't), they all allow you to do the following:

- ▶ Check in
- ▶ Find places close by
- ▶ See nearby places where your friends have checked in recently
- ▶ Send out shouts
- ▶ Add tips and notes

▶ See who is at a particular venue

▶ See your recent check-in history

▶ See and manage your friends

Let's take a quick look at each of the official Foursquare apps. Rather than delve into all the features of the apps, this lesson just shows what they look like and how they work.

NOTE

Although the official apps might all look different, they all work essentially the same way. Sure, there are some differences. For example, on a BlackBerry, you use a trackball instead of touching the screen to activate something. But having used all three official apps, I can say that they are all generally self-explanatory for the core functions needed to enjoy Foursquare.

Using Foursquare on an iPhone/iOS Device

Of all the native apps, I think the iPhone/iOS app is the one that *looks* the best and has the best user interface (see Figure 4.1). This isn't to say that the BlackBerry and Android apps are less capable, but the iPhone app just seems more polished than the others. The iOS app has been around the longest. Apple's app approval process famously (maybe infamously) is stringent on the quality of the apps approved. Foursquare has had more than a year of testing on the iPhone/iOS app now, and I think that maturity shows.

NOTE

Right now there is no official Foursquare app specifically for the iPad. You can still use the iPhone version, but it runs in the small iPhone size mode (unless you press the 2X button). A fully iPad-compatible Foursquare app (one that uses the full screen and resolution) is one of the most anticipated iPad apps that iPad owners are waiting for.

FIGURE 4.1   The iPhone Foursquare app.

One of the coolest features of the iPhone/iOS app is the map of where
your friends are (within a close geographic area). Because one of the reasons you likely use Foursquare is to go hang out with your friends, it's a
nice touch to see how close some of them actually are to you (see Figure
4.2). If you've ever been out and about and just wondered if any friends
were in the area to grab a coffee or a snack, the map feature is perfect.
Just tapping the map icon gives you a view of who is in the area. Zoom in
and out as you would on any map application on the iPhone/iOS. You can
tap a person's picture to see where they are and who they are with. And if
you wonder where the hot spots are for lunch or going out after work, a
quick look at the map gives you a pretty clear indication. Well, at least as
far as your friends are concerned.

NOTE

For in-depth answers to all your iPhone/iOS Foursquare app questions, be sure to check out the iPhone FAQ on the Foursquare site:
support.foursquare.com/forums/189985-iphone-faq.

FIGURE 4.2   An iPhone map showing nearby friends.

Like most other iPhone/iOS apps, with the Foursquare app, things happen when you drag or slide your finger on the screen. For example, with the BlackBerry and Android apps, to refresh your list of friends or places close by, you use a menu. However, with the iPhone app, you just put your finger on the screen and drag down. When you see Release to Refresh, you release and…you get the idea. Will the iPhone/iOS version get all the coolest features first? Probably not. As all the apps are improved, a new feature might be put into the next app that is updated; then the other apps will follow suit.

PLAIN ENGLISH: **FAQ**

FAQ (pronounced "fack") stands for *frequently asked questions*. What else would you call something that everyone asks about?

Using Foursquare on a BlackBerry

Depending on your BlackBerry, to use the Foursquare app, you might use touch or the trackball to navigate around the various parts of the app. The BlackBerry app was one of the last ones developed and has been frequently updated since its first private beta launch. Believe me, as is often the case with such software, the first private betas were nothing to write home about. I think it was the lack of a decent Foursquare app for the BlackBerry that kept me from using Foursquare much at first.

Unlike the iPhone/iOS version, the BlackBerry app has keyboard shortcuts you can use when using the app (see Figure 4.3)—things like f for your friends' recent check-ins or p for places near you. On touch-centric devices (like iPhones and many Android-based devices), having keyboard shortcuts is rather superfluous.

> **NOTE**
>
> One feature that's missing from the BlackBerry app is seeing a map of where your friends are. I'm guessing that this is just a temporary feature gap and should be coming in later versions.

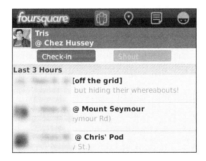

FIGURE 4.3 The Foursquare home screen on the BlackBerry.

I used the BlackBerry version for months, because I had a BlackBerry with me as a phone. It's a decent, solid app, so don't think that BlackBerry users are missing out. Foursquare has done, I think, a good job at trying to make sure that all its official apps work intuitively, quickly, and as smoothly as they can (depending on the device). One thing that is rather challenging on the BlackBerry is the shear number of different devices, screen sizes, and input methods (keyboard, touch only, keyboard and touch). This makes developing an app that works great for all devices and users difficult. As for features like maps, BlackBerry owners will have to be patient. There's a lot of people, including myself, that have been asking for it. It'll happen sooner or later.

There is a special section of the Foursquare support forums for the BlackBerry app : support.foursquare.com/forums/189989-blackberry-faq.

> **TIP**
>
> Don't hesitate to check out the FAQ for a site, a service, or an application. I check them all the time when I have a questions. When I used to work for a software company, I wrote a lot of FAQs to help people use an application. The FAQs are there for you to read and enjoy!

Using Foursquare on Android-Based Phones

The native app for Android-based devices looks much like the BlackBerry app (see Figure 4.4). However, like the iPhone app, the Android app has the map of friends feature. While both the iPhone and BlackBerry have prominent Check In buttons, the Android app does not. To check into a location on an Android device, you need to tap Places, find where you are, and then select to check in there. I think this is an unnecessary step that will be streamlined at some point.

Because you can often use Android devices either with or without a keyboard, how the app works on your particular device might depend on how you hold the device. Experimenting on a tiny (it even has *mini* in its name) device, I found the Android device to be slick and fast.

With the Android version, if the application is open in the background, it doesn't keep checking for its location until you bring it front and center. Not a big deal? Searching for the location and using the GPS all the time will suck your device's battery dry faster than a 10-year-old on a milk-shake. It's a nice touch that the developers of the Android version threw in to help save battery life. Nice. (The iPhone app works this way, too, but the BlackBerry version doesn't.)

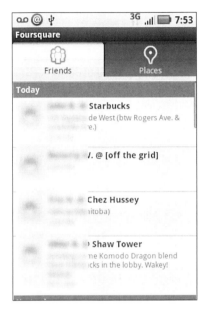

FIGURE 4.4   The Foursquare home for Android.

NOTE

Android devices could be using several different versions of the Android OS.

For more info on the Android app, check out the FAQ on the Foursquare site: support.foursquare.com/forums/189990-android-faq.

Over time, I've noticed that the three native applications are getting closer and closer together in terms of looks *and* functionality. By the time you read this book, you might be wondering what I'm talking because by then the applications might be essentially identical.

Why Aren't All the Apps the Same?

This is a very good question. It would seem that it would be easy to make sure all the same features (such as the map of friends) are available across many devices. And it would seem that all the apps would be equally easy to use. The fact of the matter is that all three devices require different programming languages and development procedures. For the iPhone, applications have to be approved by Apple before they appear in the App Store. This discourages frequent developer updates, so Apple applications seem to remain stagnant longer. The BlackBerry is unique in that there are many different version of both the hardware (phones) and the software that runs them (the operating system). Android devices are relatively new on the scene, and development of those applications has taken time to ramp up. If you add all this together, you can see why even the "official" versions of the Foursquare application are so different from device to device.

Third-Party Foursquare Apps

Like many other web-based applications today, Foursquare offers programmers an API they can use to develop *their own* apps for Foursquare. Third-party developers have made apps for Palm devices, new games based on Foursquare, and apps specifically for the iPad (but not an official iPad app). There's even an app to help you avoid your ex while you're out on the town. Like all other applications built by fans, some of the ones for Foursquare are good, and some aren't. The important thing to understand is that some of the apps are there to support other devices (such as Palm devices), while others are there to extend Foursquare to do more interesting things.

One of the growing areas of focus is expanding Foursquare's game aspect. Maybe you'd be interested in an app that would let you check into a location with a special "scavenger hunt" app for other prizes. How about a self-guided tour app that would allow you check into the stops along the way and then to get an audio program about the location? Such apps are possible. Hmm, maybe I should start working on my own app for coffee places of Vancouver....

Using the Basic Mobile Website Instead of an App

Instead of using a platform-specific app, you can always use m.foursquare.com. When I first joined Foursquare, there wasn't an app for the BlackBerry (official or not), so I did all my checking in on the mobile site. It isn't gorgeous, but it is certainly functional. Sometimes the simplicity of the mobile website might be just the thing you need (see Figure 4.5).

FIGURE 4.5   The Foursquare mobile website might be plain and simple, but it just plain works.

> **CAUTION**
>
> Yes, if you're clever, you can log into the mobile website from your computer and check in. But do you really want to do that? The folks at Foursquare are putting more and more resources into trying to cut down on cheating (especially checking into places where you clearly are not). Will there be penalties for cheating? That remains to be seen, but you don't want to find out, you do?

From the mobile website you can do all the basic Foursquare tasks. There are few images, as you can see, so it loads quickly even when you don't have the greatest connection in the world. I have to say, though, that it's one of those "better than a sharp stick in the eye" kinds of tools. It works. It's not pretty, but it works.

Checking in via SMS (U.S. Only)

I've saved the most basic way to use Foursquare for last. Not only is it simple and basic, it also works only in the United States. The method I'm talking about is sending an SMS to Foursquare.

If you don't have a mobile device that can get online—for example, if you have a regular cell phone without Internet access—you can send a text to 50500 with a message like " @ Main Street Theatre! Catching a great flick" to check in. In the next lesson, you see why this could be a hit-or-miss way to check in. In Lesson 5, you learn the ins and outs of checking in, and you'll see why having to guess at what a location is called could be a problem. (Like, for example, "Starbucks" because there could be several "Starbucks" even within a few blocks of you!)

Summary

Foursquare created or supported several "official" apps for the three most popular types of smartphones available: iPhones/iOS, BlackBerry, and Android phones. Though the official apps might look a little different from each other, they function in essentially the same way. You can also download and try one of several third-party, unofficial Foursquare apps that can add other elements of fun to using Foursquare. Lastly, if all else fails, you can always go to m.foursquare.com and use the mobile website to locate software for your specific phone.

Checking In

In this lesson you learn the critical part of Foursquare: checking in. If you don't master checking in, you can't become mayor, earn badges, or get specials. Good thing checking in is as simple as tapping or clicking.

Methods for Checking In

Checking in is probably the most important part of Foursquare. Good thing it's also the simplest task. In this lesson you learn how to do the following:

- ▶ Make sure Foursquare has you where you think you are. (Don't laugh.)

- ▶ Check into a location already in the Foursquare database.

- ▶ Check into a location new to Foursquare.

- ▶ Add some additional information about a venue.

- ▶ Send a shout-out to Twitter or Facebook.

You can do all these things on all the Foursquare mobile apps as well as on the mobile version of the Foursquare website. Remember that checking in from your laptop isn't supported—unless you use the mobile version on your laptop—but we've talked about that, haven't we?

Finding Your Location

The various Foursquare apps try to do a good job of figuring out where you are, but they are far from perfect. Even if you have a GPS in your smart phone (iPhone, Blackberry, and so on.), the GPS receiver needs time to acquire a lock on your location. Sometimes you can't get a good GPS lock no matter what. In those cases, Foursquare uses the next best thing: mobile phone towers.

Most location services have worked for years by using triangulation with three or more mobile phone towers to try to figure out where you are. The accuracy of this method ranges from a few hundred feet up to a mile. This method is called assisted GPS (AGPS). By using places that have a fixed location (mobile phone towers and WiFi networks mapped by Google Street View), your mobile device can get a good idea of where you are.

Foursquare does the best it can, but sometimes it gets confused. For example, here in Vancouver, one of our subway lines has cell service the entire time it's underground. It does this by using a cell repeater starting at the southern end of the line. Foursquare doesn't know this, so it often thinks I'm several miles away from where I actually am when I'm on or near the subway. This is because the Foursquare app is still using the AGPS location information from the repeater down the line and not one close to me. Eventually the app and my phone figure things out and get me located in the correct spot.

There are a few ways to handle Foursquare not having an accurate location for you. First, you can search for the location where you *actually* are and check in there regardless of where Foursquare thinks you are. (This doesn't trigger cheating flags; more on cheating later in this lesson.) Second, you can quit the app and restart it when you are outside and in a more open area. Third, you can switch to the Places screen and select Refresh from the menu. Perhaps a fourth option is to just wait until the GPS gets a better lock on your location and let Foursquare use that instead. In a city, sometimes that can mean a long wait. Sometimes a device might not get a good GPS lock on your position if you are surrounded by tall buildings or in a deep valley. The GPS needs to "see" and connect to the satellites that provide the location information.

Use the Places screen in your Foursquare app to see where Foursquare *thinks* you are. You can't look at a map per se, but you *can* look at the addresses of places, and at the bottom of the screen (on Blackberry, iPhone, and Android apps anyway), you'll see something like "Near 1638 Robson St, Vancouver," which gives you a general idea of where the app is placing you (see Figure 5.1).

FIGURE 5.1   The Places screen (in this case, on an Android phone).

NOTE

If you were to try to check in at the same time using two or three different devices, you might find that Foursquare places you in wildly different places. This happens because each of the devices figures out where you are a little differently. An iPad using only Wi-Fi uses Google's information from Street View to figure out where you're connected and therefore where you are(roughly). A Blackberry goes by cell towers most of the time. An Android device…well, I don't know what the one I tested was defaulting to, but it was different as well. Don't worry. Foursquare knows that there is a fudge factor in locations. It won't flag you for cheating because your device is confused!

So if you're trying to check into your favorite place, and Foursquare doesn't list it, remember that Foursquare might just think you're somewhere else. It's okay, we all feel that way sometimes.

Checking Into an Existing Location

Now that you know how to figure out *where* you are, you're ready to try checking in there. On the Blackberry and iPhone apps, the button or link for checking in is at the top. On the mobile site, it's at the bottom. If you're an Android user, you need to go to Places and choose the place before you can check in.

When you click the Check-In Here button on a smart phones, Foursquare brings up a list of places that are close by, with some of your favorite haunts at the top of the list (refer to Figure 5.1). Checking in is as simple as selecting the place from the list and then clicking Check-In Here (see Figure 5.2).

FIGURE 5.2   On the check-in screen on the iPhone, clicking the green Check-In Here button lets you check in.

As mentioned earlier, if you can't find the place you're looking for, you can try searching for the name or address of the place. Alternatively, if your friends have already checked in there, too, you can click the name of one of those friends in your list of friends, click where that person is (assuming that you're there, too), and then check in. When you do this, you're also telling Foursquare that you're "checking in with" that friend, meaning you're hanging out with that person and not just there together by coincidence. If you *still* can't find the place where you are, it might be time to add a venue, which I'll talk about in a moment.

If you've found the place where you want to check in, you're ready to press that Check-In Here button. At this point, you are presented with some choices. If you want to let all your Foursquare friends know where you are, you should make sure Tell My Friends is checked. If you've connected your Twitter and Facebook accounts to your Foursquare account, you can have your check-in broadcast there, too (see Figure 5.3).

> **NOTE**
>
> Unchecking Tell My Friends marks your check-in as "off the grid." Checking in off the grid still counts in Foursquare, but your location is kept secret.

FIGURE 5.3   Checking in on a Blackberry, with the optional Shout box and boxes to send alerts to Twitter and Facebook.

CAUTION

This is another note on privacy and safety. Depending on your Facebook and Twitter settings, by sending your Foursquare check-ins there, you might be broadcasting your location to the world. Most people keep their Twitter accounts open, and Google indexes Twitter. And if your Twitter account is not private, anyone can see what you're putting up there.

Facebook is a different story, but it's easy for your various updates to be public there as well. So, before you post a check-in to Twitter or Facebook, ask yourself whether you want the world to know where you are (or are not) right now. My choice is usually no. I keep a much closer rein on my friends on Foursquare than I do on other social networks. If I broadcast where I'm checking into on Twitter or Facebook, I might be telling far more people where I am than I really want to.

Regardless of the boxes you check on the Check-In screen, you can also add a shout like "At my favorite cafe and loading up on caffeine and sugar!" or "Going to check out the new dinosaur exhibit at the museum." Shouts add a little context, humor, or whatever to your Foursquare check-ins. I'll talk a little more about shouts (and tips) in Lesson 8.

When you check in, you get a nice little confirmation message stating that you've successfully checked in and how many points you received for it. You'll also see who the mayor is—it could be you already, or you might have just stolen it from someone—and what other notes Foursquare users have provided for the area.

This is pretty much all you have to do to check in. You've arrived, your friends can see where you are, and you've earned some points. This may not seem like much to you. But believe me, we're only starting to scratch the surface of what Foursquare can do for you.

Checking Into a New Location

Say that you've arrived at a location and want to check in, but what if the place where you *are* isn't *there*. That is, what if the location where you'd like to check in isn't in the Foursquare locations list? It's easy: You just add it! Since the launch of Foursquare in Vancouver in 2009, we mere mortals have been able to add locations to Foursquare (a privilege once reserved for the vaunted "superuser"). Doing this is simple and takes only a moment—and you get bonus points for doing it, too!

First, you should make absolutely sure that your location isn't already in Foursquare. Search on the name and the address, and then check the map. Then double-check. Foursquare tries to keep its database of listings as duplicate free as possible. (And it's an uphill battle, I'm sure.) Having duplicate locations or venues isn't a big deal, it just gets a little confusing for people picking which venue is the "right" one.

Next, when you're at the blank "not found" screen, you select the option to add a new venue. When you're adding the venue, try to be as thorough as possible. Add the address, cross street, phone number, website,...as much info you can above and beyond the name (see Figure 5.4). This not only helps people find the location using Foursquare but can also help the venue get found on the Internet as well.

> **NOTE**
>
> If you make a mistake while entering a location, don't worry. You can edit the location later.

FIGURE 5.4 Adding a new location in Foursquare.

No, you don't become mayor of the location when you first create it. I'll talk more about mayorships in the next lesson, but the basic rule is that you have to check in at least twice and more than anyone else, and you have to do so on different days. It seems a bit unfair that you can't become mayor immediately, I know, but you still get the extra points. (You'll learn more in Lesson 8.)

Additional Check-In Information: Shouts and Tweets

I mentioned earlier in the lesson that you can send out shouts when you check in. Let me explain this concept in a little more detail now. The idea is that when you check in, sometimes adding a little more info gives the check-in context humor, or it gives your audience just a little insight. Are shouts required? Not by a long shot. Do I send out a shout whenever I check in? Nope. So, if shouts aren't required, and I don't use them all the time, why bother?

Remember that Foursquare is meant to be fun. Shouts are part of the informal fun of Foursquare. I usually add a shout when I'm also adding a check-in to Twitter or Facebook. Sometimes I'm checking into a conference or seeing a friend speak or going to a concert. I think these types of check-ins are worth sharing and celebrating a bit, and a shout is a good way to do just that. So, send a shout! Share the fun.

Cheating

One of the early problems with Foursquare was a small but consistent problem of people cheating. People were checking into places where they weren't actually located. This doesn't seem like a big problem, except that it was rather disconcerting to people who were there (and had earned mayorships by visiting regularly). And it's no fun when someone is cheating in a game!

Foursquare saw the early cheating as a potential problem and started trying to confirm that people were reasonably close to where they were checking in. The folks at Foursquare keep how the anticheating system works a closely held secret, but they did share that the system looks at the *pattern* of check-ins. If you're consistently checking into places in the same general area, it's a good bet that those check-ins are all legit. However, if you start checking into places all over the globe, that might be suspicious. At this point, how successful has it been? Foursquare says it has had some great success, but it's always working on improving the system.

Now, what about when Foursquare thinks you're one place and you're really somewhere else (like when I check in at the train station when Foursquare thinks I'm miles away)? Foursquare has that covered. Given that cell towers can have potentially *huge* ranges of location results (I've had maps place me in the middle of rivers or the ocean because of this margin of error), Foursquare can't be too tough on people.

Again, what Foursquare is looking for is a *pattern* of check-ins over time. Say that you check into a place in Las Vegas, then Boston, and then Dallas over a couple hours. Yeah, unless your name is Clark Kent, that isn't going to be possible. So say that I check into the train station downtown, then a couple other places downtown, and then a place close to home. Even if Foursquare doesn't have me *exactly* in all those places, the *pattern* of my check-ins matches up with reality.

Here's the bottom line: Foursquare expects you to be honest when you're checking into a place. If your friends always see that you're at the Eiffel Tower when you live in Topeka, Foursquare really isn't helping them hang out with you. So, let's just keep it clean, folks.

Summary

Checking into locations is a pretty simple thing. Really, the Foursquare app does most of the work locating where you are and what's close to you. Just find the location or venue that you want to check into and you're off. If you've found a new place to hang out, feel free to add it. Just make sure that you provide lots of info for others to know what location you're talking about. Oh and remember, no cheating!

LESSON 6

Badges

In this lesson you learn what the deal is with Foursquare badges—how you earn them, what they mean, and what special things they can unlock. The best thing about badges is probably the most frustrating—you don't know when you're going to get them or how you did it until you get them.

Badge Basics

Games have prizes, right? You achieve something and then you get some kind of reward or token to mark the occasion. Foursquare follows this pattern, and it calls those achievements *badges*. Some badges are silly or tongue-in-cheek—like Photobooth for checking into three places that have photo booths or Jobs for checking into an Apple Store three times. Others—like Newbie for your first check-in and Super Mayor for holding 10 mayorships at once—represent more tangible goals. What are all the Foursquare badges? Well, honestly, no one outside Foursquare really knows. There are a few that we know about because lots of people have unlocked them, but others are secret—at least until you unlock them! Okay, Foursquare badges aren't a *huge* secret, but you aren't going to get much help from the Foursquare site on how to earn the various badges. I'll explain this in a bit more detail in a moment, but first let's talk about what the badges *mean*.

Is there some deep, dark secret meaning to the Foursquare badges? Is there some secret Internet society that protects the Internet, and you gain access only by earning a special combination of Foursquare badges? Nope, sorry. What you see in Figure 6.1 is pretty much it.

Badges are really just a fun way to recognize people *doing* things in Foursquare. Whether it's the Superstar badge for checking into 50 different places or the Local badge when you've been to the same place three times in a week, badges are a way for Foursquare to show how people are using the system.

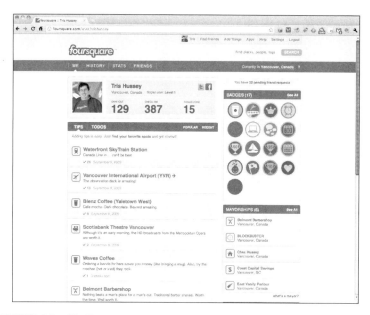

FIGURE 6.1   My Foursquare profile and my crop of badges.

Badges are about bragging rights, too.

If the badges were just for you to enjoy, do you think they'd be *on your profile page*? No, badges are also about showing other people how active you are on Foursquare. Sure, the silly ones like Player Please are funny, but checking into 50 different places or being mayor of 10 places at once or getting badges tied to special events like conferences? Those are fun and cool. Don't forget—especially as we get to later lessons on how businesses are using Foursquare—that Foursquare is supposed to be *fun*. The idea is to have fun finding new places to visit in your city or finding the places your friends like to go. Badges are an extension of this fun; a badge gives you a little icon that matches an achievement.

As Foursquare becomes more popular, more and more specific badges are being created for cities, events, and even TV shows. Here in Vancouver you can earn a special TRANSIT Champion badge for checking into a number of different major transit stations (see Figure 6.2). In New York City, Pennsylvania, and San Francisco, there are special badges as well. In

Lesson 9 I talk more about the special badges offered by brands like Bravo, MTV, TLC, and Starbucks. For now, just keep concentrating on checking in, and before you know it, you'll earn badges.

Isn't There a List of Foursquare Badges *Somewhere*?

As the folks at Foursquare concede, a little Googling goes a long way toward finding all the possible Foursquare badges out there (and some that aren't active anymore). Two of the best lists I found (with a little help from Google) are tonyfelice.wordpress.com/foursquare/ and www.4squarebadges.com/foursquare-badge-list/.

Now, I don't provide this information so you can go out on a badge-collecting spree. I think looking at the badges, especially the ones from the South By Southwest conference (SXSW) and from Bravo, gives you a look into how Foursquare *could* be used in the future. Until then, don't tell anyone I told you about these sites. It's our little secret.

FIGURE 6.2 Vancouver's special TRANSIT Champion badge for checking in and using the public transit system.

Earning Your First Badge

Your first badge is the Newbie badge, which you receive for your first
check-in after you create your account. Yeah, everyone has that one.
You'll get an email and a notification when it happens. What happens
then? Well, not very much until you start checking in at more places. The
next badge you're likely to scoop up is the Local badge for three check-
ins in the same place in a week (see Figure 6.3).

FIGURE 6.3   The Local badge. Yep, I got it.

After that, you're likely to get the Adventurer badge for checking in at 10
different places. From there on out, the rest are up to you!

How often should you expect to earn new badges? Probably not often.
Like mayorships, badges are getting harder to come by. Some of them,
like Gossip Girl, involve arcane rules about where and when you need to
check in. Badges are becoming quite a treasure hunt, which, actually, I
enjoy.

> **NOTE**
>
> It would be fun if Foursquare allowed people to create online scavenger hunts for badges for occasions, events, or just the heck of it. Sure, Foursquare does it for big conferences, but I'd like to do it for myself, too.

Swarms

How many people were at your last party? What if you threw a party and everyone checked into Foursquare at your place? Well, if there were 50 or more people, everyone who checked in would unlock the Swarm badge (see Figure 6.4).

FIGURE 6.4   My friend Reg and his Swarm badge.

The key with the Swarm badge is that it's not just for 50 people checking in at the same place over the course of a day or week. Rather, they have to check in within a three-hour span. This badge is special because it applies to large events. Recognizing this fact, businesses have launched Foursquare Swarm events by offering specials and such. These swarms have ended up bringing in tremendous amounts of business. Think about it: If you can get an influx of people to come into your business in three hours, that's pretty good.

If checking in with 50 people isn't enough for you, how about earning the Super Swarm badge? You get that when you're one of 250 people or more who check in at the same place at the same time (see Figure 6.5). For SXSW, Foursquare created this badge because Foursquare users were hitting 50-person swarms without batting an eye.

> **NOTE**
>
> Foursquare launched at SXSW in 2009 and had a huge presence there in 2010. South by Southwest (SXSW) is one of the biggest tech, music, and film conferences in the United States.

FIGURE 6.5 My friend John and his Super Swarm badge earned at SXSW 2010.

Special Event Badges

Holding a conference and want people to check in at various specific activities? Foursquare can create a special badge (or badges) just for your event. To date, there haven't been many private or small-party badges created (that we know of), but there have been several badges created for tech and sports events. Here's the thing to remember about Foursquare badges: Sometimes you don't know they're out there until you unlock them!

> **NOTE**
>
> If you want your own event badge, contact Foursquare through the Foursquare website.

The best way to find Foursquare badges is to keep an eye on your Foursquare friends' activity streams. I have Foursquare set to post to Facebook and Twitter whenever I unlock a new badge (or become mayor of a location). If I manage to earn a special badge, my Facebook friends and those who follow me on Twitter will know about it!

> **TIP**
>
> If you're at a conference, try to see if you can check into the conference as a location instead of checking into the physical location where the convention is held; for example, try to check into the Web 2.0 Expo instead of the Moscone Center. If you don't see the event on your list, you can look for it by searching for places.
>
> If you see that one of your friends has checked into the same place, you can click his or her name, then the place, and check in with the person. Using this method might help to unlock a Swarm badge and unlock some special event badge for both you and your friend.

Summary

For a big part of the Foursquare game, badges are a huge mystery for all but the people at Foursquare. Although some badges like, Barrista (for checking into a lot of different Starbucks) and On A Boat (for being on some boat-like thing), make sense, a lot of them don't. If you are looking to Foursquare to shed some light on the situation, don't hold your breath. Everything points to Foursquare keeping badges and how you earn them as the secret part of the game.

Becoming a Mayor

In this lesson, you learn all about one of the most entertaining parts of Foursquare—becoming mayor of locations. There's a little more to it than just showing up, and there is more to be had than just the title.

What Is a Mayor?

Ah, it's good to be a king—or in Foursquare's case, a mayor. The *mayor* of a location is the person who checks in there the most. Now, before you start wandering down to your favorite lunch place and checking in every hour, know that it doesn't quite work that way. First, only your first check-in on a day counts. Check in twice in one day, and you get credit for only one check-in. In addition, you have to have a profile picture to be the mayor of *anywhere*. Hmm, that seems odd. Or does it? Well, you don't have to wait long to find out because that's what this lesson is all about: becoming, and staying, mayor.

You know when you go to a place often enough that your special made-to-order latte is started when you open the door. I think we all like to go, as the song goes, where everyone knows your name. Well, Foursquare thinks there should be a reward, and competition, for the frequent visitors to a location. Now, I'm saying *location* because, as you might have figured out by now, "location" is a fluid concept on Foursquare. The grocery store is a location. A train station is a location. A bus stop or even a bus *route* can be a location on Foursquare. And your office or cubicle can be a location.

So, being mayor of a place…well, it's about who goes there the most. When you check into a location, Foursquare tells you who's the mayor of the place. But is this little bit of recognition all that's involved in being mayor. For now, yes. But it's becoming a lot more than that. Before we get into why it's good to be mayor, let's talk about becoming one in the first place.

How to Become the Mayor of a Location

Becoming the mayor of a location is simple: You just go there and check in the most. But what does Foursquare mean by *most*? This is the catch. Checking in every hour doesn't gain you anything. Nor does trying to cheat by checking into a different location from home. The visits count on a once-per-day basis. So, even if you go to the same store twice in one day, only one visit counts toward becoming mayor. Yes, you still earn points for both visits, but you don't get extra credit toward a mayorship. You have to go to a place twice, with the two visits on different days, as a minimum for being mayor.

A mayorship is given to the user with the most check-ins in the past 60 days (see Figure 7.1). So, for example, say that you check in Monday and Tuesday at a new venue where no one else has checked in at least twice. You'll be mayor…until someone checks in there Wednesday, Thursday, and Friday *and* you haven't checked in since Tuesday (giving them three days to your two). Nice, huh?

FIGURE 7.1   You can see I've been to a local movie-rental place twice in the past 60 days, but I'm only one day away from becoming mayor!

You can see how competition can heat up over mayorships. A friend of mine "stole" the mayorship from me at my second office (aka coffee shop), so I had to steal it back from him. It took some time, too. And then I got him back: I ousted him as mayor of Dairy Queen. Ousting mayors? Yep, now this is fun.

Becoming mayor is, in some respects, like earning a badge because it happens without warning. You check in as usual at the laundromat, but you've been there a couple extra times this week, and you're greeted with a cheerful "Congratulations, you've just become Mayor of Suds-n-Such Laundromat!" or a variant of that message saying you've ousted someone as mayor of that location (see Figure 7.2). When people check in there, they'll see that *you* are now the mayor. In addition, Suds-n-Such will now be listed on your profile under your mayorships. Like most other things in Foursquare, it's rather simple: You go somewhere the most, and you become mayor of the location.

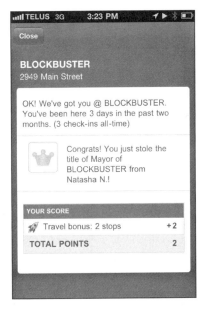

FIGURE 7.2   Yes, I went back the next day to become mayor of the movie-rental store. The movie had to go back, you know.

The Picture Requirement

Before I move on to talk about ousting mayors, I want to touch on one requirement for being a mayor: You must have a Foursquare profile picture. You might think this sounds strange, but there are two things at work here. First, it's unlikely that a spammer would take the time to upload a picture to a fake profile and then start checking into a place enough to be mayor. (And remember that you have to be located close to the venue to check in, so there is that protection as well.) Second, Foursquare *does* want to encourage businesses to get involved in people becoming mayors and give them "mayoral perks." Including a picture helps businesses recognize you.

If you have a picture on your profile, you are eligible for mayorships. And if you set your privacy settings to allow businesses to see that you check in with them, smart business owners might offer you perks. For example, the person behind the counter at your favorite lunch spot might recognize you and say, "Hey, look! It's the new mayor of Luigi's Sandwiches! A free sandwich for you today!" Smart, huh? If you don't have a picture, how would the shop know you're the mayor?

> NOTE
>
> Technically you could have a silly picture on your profile that isn't actually you, but I'm just not going to go there.

Being Ousted as Mayor of a Location

So, you've checked into Luigi's more days than anyone else, and now you're the mayor. Then one day you get an email saying "Sorry for the bad news, but Jill S. has ousted you as mayor of Luigi's Sandwiches." Wait! What? I'm loyal, I go there every day for my lunch. Okay, I missed Tuesday, but.... You've been ousted as mayor (see Figure 7.3).

If your ego just can't stand the hit of losing a mayorship, there's only one road open to you: Keep making return visits to the location until you're back on top.

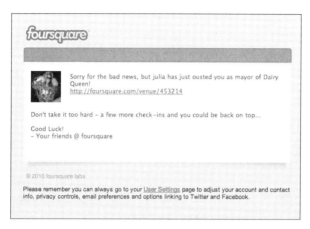

FIGURE 7.3   The email letting me know that I was no longer mayor of Dairy Queen.

Ousting the Current Mayor

Okay, so you frequently go to your local grocery store and dutifully check in every time. Every time you check in, you see that Sue L. is *still* the mayor of the store. Then one day you see "Congrats! You just stole the title of Mayor of Superfoods from Sue L.!" How'd that happen? Simply, you visited the store and checked in more than Sue did. But Sue might oust you soon. You have to keep going there—and checking in—*more* than she does.

> NOTE
> Remember that just going to a location doesn't count toward earning a mayorship. Foursquare doesn't know you're there unless you check in.

Ousting someone as mayor of a location sounds simple. But as Foursquare is become more popular, it's actually getting *harder* to snatch that title away from someone. When Foursquare first launched, there weren't many users. At that point, there might have been only two or three people going to a place who were even *using* Foursquare; many people hadn't even heard of it. It's not hard to be mayor when the competition is nil.

Once a few dozen people are all vying for mayor—and technically, everyone is vying for mayor just by checking in—it gets a lot harder to get enough check-ins to be number one and stay that way. In my neighborhood, there are a few places where people check in a lot and where I'm in competition with several folks for mayor. I think I'd have to go to the grocery store (for example) every day for a solid week to oust the current mayor, who is not only a friend of mine but also works around the corner from the store. I just don't shop for groceries that often. On the flip side, I'm still mayor of my house.

Gaining mayorships is going to become *even more difficult* when businesses begin offering real mayoral perks. I don't *always* remember to check into the store when I go, but if I got 10% off my grocery bill for the entire time I was mayor, you can bet I'd make sure I'd check in every time I went there. Actually, if that perk existed, maybe my wife would stop bugging me when I check into the store as we're walking in. Then again, I'd probably wind up doing all the grocery shopping. Well, this all leads to an important question: Are there perks for being a mayor?

Perks of Being the Mayor of a Location

It's good to be king, but is there really any point to being mayor? Well, yes and no. Some businesses jumped right on the Foursquare bandwagon. Here in Vancouver, the Blenz coffee chain offered benefits to the mayors of its locations almost as soon as Foursquare was activated in Vancouver. Each mayor received a $5 gift card for becoming mayor.

Blenz is active in social media, offering gift cards and contests not only through Foursquare but Twitter as well. If a small business wants to look at examples of companies leveraging Foursquare to get more people into their stores, Blenz is a great place to start.

As another example, Starbucks ran a promotion in 2010, offering $1 off its Frappuccino drinks to the mayor of a Starbucks location. I was one of the lucky participants in this promotion while I was mayor of my local Starbucks. But I experienced the same problem as many other people when Starbucks made this offer, which lasted quite a long time.

With Starbucks locations everywhere, for months we saw "Special Nearby" banners when we checked into places, and it wasn't clear where the special was. This was detrimental to other businesses because after a while, people stopped checking the specials.

Offering perks to Foursquare mayors and other users is starting to catch on, and businesses are developing better techniques for doing so. Mayors are getting perks like a free coffee a day or a free appetizer. Some places offer specials just for checking in—not only for the mayor. These perks tie into a key aspect of Foursquare and mayorships: loyalty. Offering mayoral perks is just the beginning, and some businesses are starting to get pretty innovative.

> NOTE
>
> I'll talk more about how businesses are getting involved with Foursquare in Lesson 9.

It can be good to be mayor, so get out there and oust your local mayor. Just don't oust me from my own house. Because that would just be wrong.

Summary

If there is a benefit to Foursquare, it's becoming Mayor of a location or venue. Sure the badges we talked about in Lesson 6 are fun and all, but as more and more businesses offer benefits to the Mayor, you can see why becoming mayor could become a hotly contested office to hold. Remember, becoming mayor is just the person who *checks in* the most over the last 60 days, and you can be ousted as mayor if you don't keep going and checking in. By the way, there is even a special badge for holding down 10 mayorships at once. On to Lesson 8.

Getting More Out of Foursquare

In this lesson you learn how to get more out of Foursquare with check-in history, connecting with other social media services (like Twitter and Facebook), and using Tips.

Foursquare Is About More Than Check-Ins

By now your Foursquare profile should be all spiffy and awesome. You've checked into locations, you've maybe added a few locations, and perhaps you're the mayor of a place or two (or three). Hopefully you've done some exploring with your mobile client of choice to find all the little features that Foursquare has to offer. (I stumble on new features all the time.) This lesson talks about some of the additional features of Foursquare that make it fun and interesting.

Reviewing Your Check-In History

Whether you're accessing Foursquare from your mobile device, the mobile website, or the regular website, you can look at where you've been checking in of late through your check-in history (see Figure 8.1).

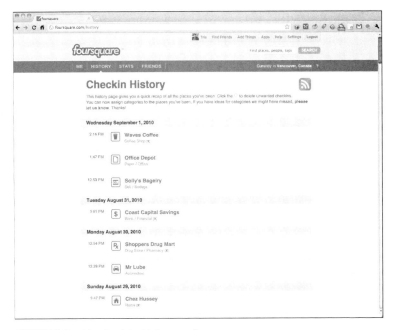

FIGURE 8.1   My check-in history on Foursquare.

There are a couple reasons you might want to check your history. For one thing, you might just be curious about where you go a lot. Also, you might want to make sure all your check-ins are accounted for and delete some.

Foursquare doesn't allow you to go back and add a check-in, but it *does* let you delete check-ins. Sometimes—though rarely—you get double-checked into a place. In such an instance, you can use your check-in history to find duplicates and remove them. Or you may have checked into a place that you'd rather not let the world know you've visited. When that happens, you can just delete the check-in for that one. Just pass your mouse over the check-in, and it will highlight in yellow, and you'll see a little "x" in a circle. Just click that and it asks you to confirm. When you click OK…that's it. The check-in is deleted.

Reviewing Your Foursquare Stats

In addition to checking your Foursquare history, you can also check other Foursquare stats (see Figure 8.2). You can look at the number of days you checked in over the past week or month. You can also look at the number of check-ins, average check-ins when you're out, percentage of check-ins at new-to-you places, and new places you've discovered. You can also look at some nice charts that show the distribution of check-ins by day of the week (do you check in most on Mondays or Thursdays?) or the days in the past month on which you checked into the most locations. You can also see which of your friends you've checked in with the most. And you can see where you've gone the most (or at least where you've checked in the most) in the past month.

FIGURE 8.2 My Foursquare stats.

How interesting this information is to you depends on how much of a data junkie you are. (I love all sorts and kinds of data, but even this is a little much for me.) Right now, there isn't much you can do with the data besides noticing, "Wow, I sure check into that donut shop a lot." But I imagine this information is going to be more and more interesting to marketers in the near future. If I were a store owner, I'd like to know the days people check in the most, and maybe even when during the day. That, however, is a discussion for Lesson 9. This lesson is still about you.

> **NOTE**
>
> Foursquare should give us the option to opt out of some parts of the data collection and make the rest anonymous. Foursquare isn't doing this yet, but I suspect that when a critical mass of users and businesses hit Foursquare it will happen. In the past Foursquare has shown that it takes its users' privacy and security seriously.

Using Your Connections to Have More Fun

You have 200 friends. So what? What good is it to know what all those people are doing? Well, you can use the tips, reviews, and shouts that your friends (and others) leave at venues when they check in to find places to go and things to do.

When you go to the Friends tab/section of your mobile Foursquare app, you can see what your friends are up to. You can sort the list by time (newest first) or distance (closest to you at the moment). If you scroll down on your list of friends, you can even see what your friends in other cities are doing. Okay, fine; if your best friend just checked into a concert that you really wanted to do go to, that isn't so great. But when you see a friend check into a place close to you that you haven't been to yet, you know you have someone to ask about that place.

Your friends (and others, of course) can leave tips and shouts about a place. These shouts and tips pop up when you check into places (see Figure 8.3). I leave tips about things like what's good on the menu or what store has good prices or a nice selection of things. If you're checking into a place like a gallery or museum, you can direct your friends to your favorite spot in that location. It's a nice touch, I think.

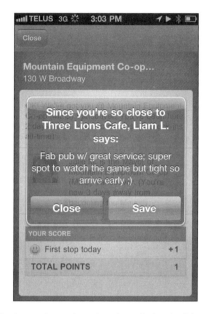

FIGURE 8.3   A tip for a place close to where I checked in.

> TIP
>
> While tips just pop up on the iPhone, on the BlackBerry you have to scroll down to see tips and other information. So don't forget to scroll! Shouts only appear in your timeline and are just bits of additional information when someone checks into a place.

Now, you can also use your friends to find *more* friends to connect with on Foursquare. Remember that connecting your profile to your Twitter and Facebook accounts doesn't just let you *broadcast* to those services; it also lets you double-check to see which friends on those services are already using Foursquare. Sure, it might seem like a little thing, but this is what I find *most* helpful about using those connections: You can connect with people you already know.

To connect with people you know on Facebook or Twitter, follow these steps:

1. Go to the main Foursquare website and log in.

2. Click Find Friends at the top of the page, close to your picture, as shown in Figure 8.4. (You did remember to put up a spiffy cool picture, didn't you?)

FIGURE 8.4 You find more friends, and people you already know who have recently joined Foursquare, the same way you added them earlier.

3. Now, just as you do when starting off with Foursquare, have Foursquare check your Facebook and Twitter friends as well as your Gmail contacts.

But wait! If you did this before, why should you do it again? Excellent question! The reason is that new people join Foursquare all the time, and it's a good idea to check every so often to see if new folks you already know are now on Foursquare.

> **NOTE**
>
> Facebook launched a similar check-in system called Places in August 2010. Places connects with Foursquare (and several other services) In the days following the launch many people on Facebook joined Foursquare, so I expect that a lot more of your Facebook friends might have Foursquare accounts now.

Checking the Leaderboard

Have I mentioned that Foursquare is a game? You get points when you check into places, but what are they good for? This is where the leaderboard comes in. The leaderboard shows you who among your friends— and who in your city overall—has earned the most points in the *past week*. So the leaderboard isn't a list of all–time-high scores. Every Monday, the leaderboard is reset, so you can see who among your friends is checking in the most and earning the most points.

When I look at my friends, I think I'm doing pretty well (see Figure 8.5). Then I look at Vancouver overall, and I realize I'm a Foursquare lightweight (see Figure 8.6). Holy smokes! Some people must check in every couple blocks!

The leaderboard is available only on mobile clients, but if you want to see this information on your laptop or desktop computer, you can go to m.foursquare.com. In fact, going to m.foursquare.com and logging in there is the easiest and fastest way I know of to check out the leaderboard. You just log in and find Leaderboard; it's number 6 on the page shown in Figure 8.7.

On the BlackBerry client, you go to the Me section and scroll down to View Leaderboard. On the iPhone client, you go to Me, tap the Me button, and then tap the square with the dots in it at the top of the menu bar; the leaderboard is at the top. On Android devices, you click the menu button, choose More and then Leaderboard.

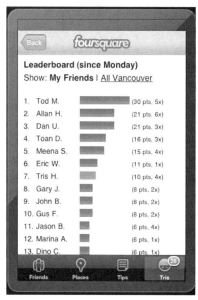

FIGURE 8.5   Foursquare leaderboard showing just my friends and me.

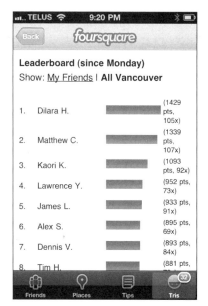

FIGURE 8.6   Foursquare leaderboard for all of Vancouver. Yeah, wow.

FIGURE 8.7 The mobile browser version of Foursquare, with a link to the Leaderboard.

Regardless of the device you use to access the leaderboard, the data you see is the same. You can look at how you're doing among your friends or against the city overall. As I said earlier, my social group must not be terribly social because we're pretty well trounced by other Foursquare users in our city.

> **NOTE**
>
> You might not think your peer group is really into Foursquare, but by looking at your city, you might be surprised to find that people are really active.

So, what's the point of the leaderboard? Right now, Foursquare is still a points game, but one of the features of Foursquare that is slated for a revamp is the "game play" aspect of earning points and such. What's coming in the future? I don't know, but I'd like to see things like the person with the most points in a day earning discounts at different places or each week's highest scorer getting some kind of badge.

> NOTE
>
> What will come remains to be seen. You can be sure that if there's something new with Foursquare, I'll have it on this book's website: www.teachyourselffoursquare.com.

Editing Locations

Humans, by nature, make mistakes. So it's not surprising that there are errors in Foursquare locations. If you've earned superuser status, or if you've added a particular venue, you can edit venue information to correct it, or you can augment it with updates. For example, say that a store's basic info is right, but the store just started using Twitter.

If you go to the location's page on the main Foursquare website and you see Edit Venue at the top of the page, above the map, you can add information for the location (see Figure 8.8).

FIGURE 8.8   I can edit the location information for this Waves shop.

If a location or venue doesn't have a category assigned to it (or if it's incorrect), you can edit the category associated with it as well as enter tags to go with the venue. Remember from Lesson 5 that tags are like keywords that go beyond a place's category. For example, a store might be categorized under Department Store, but you can add tags such as "open late" or "outlet" or "helpful staff." You can edit tags and categories if the following are all true:

▶ You are a superuser.

▶ You are the mayor of the location.

▶ You have checked into the location a specified number of times.

Taking Advantage of Foursquare Tips

All along, I've been saying that you can use Foursquare to find out what your friends suggest at venues and locations. These recommendations are called *tips*. Tips can be simple, like "Try the potato skins; they are awesome" or "Talk to Joe at the paint counter; he really knows his stuff!" Or they can be more complex, with details on the venue, such as information on finding a particularly nice spot in a park.

You can add a tip either through the mobile app or the main Foursquare website. Either way, you just go to a venue and add something to the Tips section below the map. Figure 8.9 shows the tips for my favorite burger place in Vancouver (Moderne Burger—highly, highly recommended).

TIP

Don't hold back on tips. Remember that tips are just what you'd tell friends. And they don't have to be positive. Yes, be polite, but if you think there is something important—like "stay away from the chicken"—then let people know it!

FIGURE 8.9   Tips on the location page for Moderne Burger.

When you mouse over a tip someone else has entered, you see two little check boxes: I've Done This! and Add as To-Do. Of course, if you've done what the tip says, you should select I've Done This. Commonly followed tips move up higher on the venue's profile page. On *your* profile page, you can see the tips you've entered and how many people have done *those*!

If you *haven't* already done as a tip suggests but would like to, you can select Add as To-Do, and the tip then appears on your profile page under To-Dos.

Using the To-Do Feature

To-dos are just tips that you want to do. Who doesn't want to get the inside scoop from someone and then get that awesome deal or extra-special only-if-you-ask-for-it cocktail that the bartender invented? Exactly. We all do. These sorts of things make us feel cool and in the know. So, when you come to a tip you haven't done but want to, you can mark it as a to-do, and it appears in your list of to-dos (see Figure 8.10). When you do a to-do, you can mouse over it in your list and check I've Done This! At this point, the tip loses its to-do status.

FIGURE 8.10   A list of tips I'd like to try appears in my to-dos list.

> NOTE
>
> Your to-do's remain on your profile page until you mark that you've done them.

Your profile page keeps track of both your to-do's and the to-do's you've marked as being done. Now, does doing to-do's mean you're really cool or that you know where to find the best stuff? Well maybe, but it definitely means you've figured how to tap into your Foursquare friends to find and do cool stuff!

Sending a Shout Out to Your Friends

Another useful feature in Foursquare is shouts. Typically, you shout when checking in. But you can shout whenever you like (see Figure 8.11)! You can use a shout to say just about anything in 140 characters or less (just like in Twitter). Your shouts can stay on Foursquare, or you can send them to Twitter and Facebook. It's up to you.

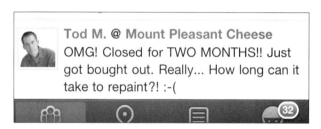

FIGURE 8.11   A friend's shout about a local place being closed for renovations.

Should you shout often? It depends on your friends and network. I tend to use Twitter for general statements. I could post from Twitter to Foursquare as well, but I don't think that's what my friends on Foursquare are following me for. I save shouts for when I'm checking in and there's something special to talk about, such as an event, a deal, or a celebration. Don't let me stifle your inner shouter, though. Feel free to use Foursquare however you want!

The Foursquare shouts that make the most sense to me are the ones that are tied to check-ins. However, not all your followers on Twitter or Facebook want to hear about all your Foursquare shouts and check-ins. To be on the safe side, use shouts judiciously, for really cool stuff. Don't forget about the boy who shouted wolf on Foursquare!

Summary

There is more to Foursquare than just badges, mayors, and checking in. As Foursquare grows in popularity, sending shouts and leaving tips (recommendations, really) might become the most interesting and vital parts of the whole system. That means it's up to us to make sure we keep the ecosystem thriving with information.

Businesses and Foursquare

This lesson covers how to claim your business with Foursquare and how businesses are starting to use Foursquare to create customers.

How Businesses Benefit from Foursquare

Throughout this book, I've been talking about Foursquare from the perspective of a *user*—a person who's going into venues, checking in, vying for mayorship, and trying to earn badges. This lesson focuses on not just users but also venue *owners*. Foursquare is useful to a number of businesses—stores, cafes, attractions, and the like—allowing them to offer specials to entice customers.

> NOTE
>
> You *can* stake a claim to your house or office on Foursquare (by becoming the manager), but Foursquare doesn't approve specials or bonuses for these types of locations.

Foursquare encourages users to check in so that they can find their friends and their friends can find them. However, Foursquare also encourages businesses to get in on the fun. Offering a check-in special or mayoral perk can get people checking in and keep them checking in over time. Sure, Foursquare is great for knowing where friends are, but there *does* have to be something else to help keep the ecosystem going. Specials and perks are the somethings, and Foursquare wants businesses to set them up. Before you can start offering a special, though, you have to claim your venue on Foursquare.

Claiming Your Venue

The first step in getting your business more involved in Foursquare is to claim your venue. First, you find your venue on Foursquare and look for the orange banner that says Do You Manage This Venue? Claim Here (see Figure 9.1). When you click on the Claim Here portion, you're taken to a page that walks you through the process of claiming your venue.

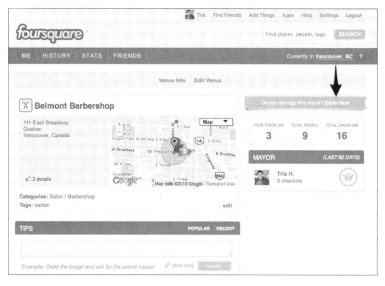

FIGURE 9.1   An unclaimed venue on Foursquare and the banner you click to claim it.

> NOTE
>
> Yes, you do have to have a Foursquare account to claim your venue. If you have a business, you may want to have two accounts: one for the business and one for yourself. It doesn't matter whether you choose to use one account or two, but you do have to have an account to get going.

You need to confirm details of the address, phone number, website address, page on Yelp.com, and page on Google Places. According to Foursquare, it takes one week to 10 days for your claim to be processed. Yes, real people do check out these claims, and a real person will be contacting you to make sure you're the legitimate person running the venue.

For more information on the process of claiming a venue, see Foursquare's business section (foursquare.com/businesses/) and help section (support.foursquare.com/forums/177952-foursquare-for-business). After your claim is processed and you hold the keys to your Foursquare kingdom, you can start creating specials, bonuses, and perks. Before you do that, you might want to take one more step, though: Identify who works at your venue.

Identifying Your Venue's Manager and Employees

People work at venues, and it wouldn't be fair to your patrons if the *employees* of a place could become mayor. They *have* to be there almost every day, and customers go there when they need or want something—and generally spend money at the venue. So one of the first steps in managing your venue is to note who works there. In your venue management page, you add the Foursquare IDs of your employees so that they won't be eligible for perks, specials, or mayorships.

> **NOTE**
>
> Your employees don't have to worry about privacy because their profiles don't appear linked to the venue page. It's only a backend housekeeping kind of thing to make sure that employees don't have an unfair advantage over customers.

You add employees in your venue management section on Foursquare. You just need to enter the employees' IDs, and Foursquare takes care of the rest.

Checking Your Venue's Analytics

I know you're chomping at the bit to get into specials and offers, but let's talk data first. Once you're managing your venue on Foursquare, you get access to the following analytics about your venue:

- ▶ Most recent visitors

- ▶ Most frequent visitors

- ▶ Time of day people check in

- ▶ Total number of unique visitors

- ▶ Histogram of check-ins per day

- ▶ Gender breakdown of customers

- ▶ Portion of Foursquare check-ins broadcast to Twitter and Facebook

Examining this data is your first step in determining what kind of offers you want to give. For example, if you want to encourage repeat business, offering a deal on the first and third check-in would be a good idea. Or maybe you want to offer a special tied to a certain time of day.

You can use the data Foursquare provides to learn about a particular segment of your clientele. Depending on your city, Foursquare users might be technology early adopters, or they might be closer to the mainstream. Here in Vancouver, Foursquare got a great start with the launch party, and it's growing steadily, but it's still a niche offering for an early adopter and web-savvy crowd. This isn't a bad thing by any stretch because early adopters are often the people who make great evangelists for new products, services, *and businesses*.

Knowing the check-in patterns for your business can start to give you insight into your customers—at least a slice of them.

Specials and Offers

Foursquare gives you a range of specials to offer people when they check in:

▶ **Check-in specials**—A user unlocks this type of special by checking into your venue at a certain time.

▶ **Frequency-based specials**—A user unlocks this type of special after a particular number of check-ins.

▶ **Wildcard specials**—These specials are always unlocked, but your staff has to verify some extra conditions before awarding them.

When you create a special, it doesn't go live right away; Foursquare has to approve it first. This is what the Foursquare help documentation says about its approval process for specials and perks: "Generally speaking, we have two main criteria for specials which we look for during the approval process: (1) does the special provide value (usually economic) to users? and (2) is this special unique to foursquare users who check in at your venue?"

> NOTE
>
> When you're running a special that is time-sensitive, make sure to deactivate it when the special is done. Customers get annoyed when they see a great special that expired a month ago.

Check-In Offers

One of the keys to creating check-in offers is to make them valuable to users who are checking in. Perks need to be valuable (generally in the economic sense) and exclusive to Foursquare users. The offer "Special nearby: Free smile to everyone who checks in at our place!" won't be valuable to most folks. (I hope you smile at everyone, regardless of whether they're using Foursquare!) However, something like "Show your check-in and get a large coffee for the price of a small" *is* valuable to a lot of users *and* something that is just for Foursquare users.

NOTE

An extra 10% off the purchase price and a free reusable bag are other examples of specials or offers. Offers that I haven't seen very often but really like are the frequency-based ones (for example, a free muffin with your coffee every third check-in).

How do people know if your business is offering a special? The Foursquare app puts a nice orange Special button next to a nearby venue that's offering a special (see Figure 9.2). If a customer is checking into a place with a special, he or she sees the Special Here button at the top of the screen, as in Figure 9.3. When the customer select this special on the screen, the text of the special appears; Figure 9.4 shows an example of a special.

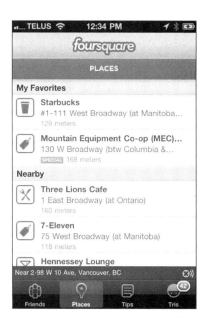

FIGURE 9.2   A special offer in the Places list on an iPhone.

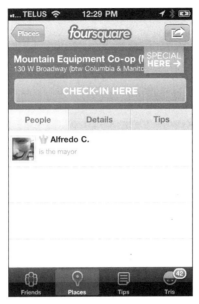

FIGURE 9.3   The Special Here button when checking into a location on an iPhone.

FIGURE 9.4   A special offer on an iPhone.

If a user is checking into a place that has a special close by, he or she sees the Special Nearby button in the corner instead of Special Here. Selecting this button gives the customer information about the special so she can decide whether it's worth going to that venue.

As you can see from Figure 9.4, a special must be brief. Mobile devices don't offer a lot of real estate for specials, and users are generally on the go while reading them, so it's important to keep specials short and to the point.

If you specify rules with a special, Foursquare handles some rules for you; for example, if it takes three check-ins to unlock a special, Foursquare manages that for you. The only time you need to worry about human intervention on the venue side of the operation is if the special is something like "Show your check-in at check-out for a 10% discount." In that case, you should make sure that all your employees know about the special, what the rules are, and what Foursquare is before the special goes live. Customers who see a special but can't use it because an employee isn't familiar with the promotion are likely to be frustrated with the venue.

Mayoral Perks

Another type of special you should consider offering is something for your mayor. Obviously, you can be as generous as you want, but I think offering "all the coffee you can drink" might be a little extreme. Perks such as "a free cup of coffee" or "a pint of beer" or "a free dessert" will encourage your mayor to come back and visit you again. Chances are that the mayor is already planning to return, given that this is the person that has been to your venue the most in the last couple months. But it's nice to reward your loyal customers and keep them spreading the word about your venue.

Yes, there have been some amazing mayor prizes, such as a free trip or free sandwiches for a year, but businesses tend to offer such extravagant prizes as a way to get media coverage. In general, you should make your mayoral perks simple but nice. I'm the mayor of several local coffee places, and if one of them offered me a free muffin with my coffee when I came in, the place would probably get the lion's share of my business. If the mayoral perk is good enough, it will encourage people to check in more often and maybe get some competition going for the mayorship.

> **NOTE**
>
> Competition is a good thing, and you can use your analytics to get some insight about how to drum up competition.

Maybe you could offer a big perk or prize for the person who is the mayor the most during a certain time period. What you offer is up to you, but it does have to comply with Foursquare's guidelines for special offers. So, offering the mayor an *extra* big smile still doesn't cut it as a perk.

Who's Offering Perks?

You might be wondering who else is offering perks in your area and what they're offering. If you go to the Foursquare business page, you can see a selection of offers from around your area. While writing this lesson, for example, I saw the following offers in and around Vancouver:

- ▶ **Ethical Bean Xpress**—Free cup of coffee for the mayor!

- ▶ **Aveda Institute Vancouver**—In August, check in at the Aveda Institute Vancouver and receive a complimentary Stress Relieving Ritual and a FREE Control Force Firm Hold Hair Spray sample (until Aug 31, until supplies last).

- ▶ **Video Magic Entertainment**—FREE popcorn or chocolate treats with your movie rentals when you check in. Mayor will receive a FREE movie rental on the next visit.

- ▶ **Lush**—As mayor of this store, enjoy a free 9ml bottle of Tuca Tuca fragrance! (Limit one per customer.)

▶ **The Charles Bar**—Hey it's your 1st check-in. We're giving you 20% off your entree today (drinks and dessert excluded). Wait til you see what the Mayor gets....

▶ **Steamworks Brewing Company**—Checkin @ Steamworks this weekend, email fraternizer@steamworks.com your servers name and fave Steamworks beer. We'll mail you a gift certificate for a complimentary beer on us during your next visit.

▶ **The Mill Marine Bistro and Bar**—Hey hey! Mayor receives a free beer! Show your server to redeem.

▶ **Mac Station**—Free Mac Station bag for the Mayor on the end of each month!

▶ **Capones Restaurant**—For every 5th check-in at Capones receive a free Ketel One martini for you and a friend! Show to your server to redeem.

▶ **Café Hermosa**—Free Coffee with purchase of food. Upon check-in.

▶ **American Eagle Outfitters**—Check in to any AE store and unlock a 15% Off discount towards your next merchandise purchase. Expires 9/30/10. Limit one per customer.

▶ **Invoke**—Welcome Social Media Maven. Half price websites every 3rd check-in.

▶ **Ceili's Irish Pub & Restaurant**—Your choice of pint on Ceilis for the mayor at any time, any day!

▶ **Vancouver Police Museum**—Hey Hey! Show staff you've checked in to the Police Museum and The mayor will receive a 25% discount in the gift shop, plus free admission for themselves and a guest.

▶ **Rogue Kitchen & Wetbar**—Check-in at Rogue and email us your server's name and your favourite dish to fraternizer@roguewetbar.com and we'll send you a gift card for a complimentary cocktail during your next visit!

▶ **One Saigon**—30% off all food between 3pm-5pm when you check in on Foursquare

There are several offers in this list that I'm interested in already! The businesses in this list are not all huge chains or even famous brands. Some are small businesses that are tapping into new and expanding areas of technology. No, Foursquare might not be a huge thing right now, but its further integration with Facebook in the near future will make Foursquare a great tool for marketing your business. Reward the people who come often; attract those who are in the area. It seems pretty simple to me.

> NOTE
>
> Note that some offers are available during a certain time of day. For example, One Saigon is offering a discount between 3 and 5 p.m., which is probably usually a slow time. Everyone wins when Foursquare users take advantage of this offer: The restaurant gets more business, and the customer gets a good discount on an early dinner!

Claiming your venue on Foursquare is where you need to start. Get that process completed and then work on the deals you'd like to offer. Beyond offering "in app" deals, you can also think about having a Foursquare event to drive more traffic to your venue. You could advertise a special party or something at your venue and make checking into Foursquare part of the deal. Check in to get it or something like that. These methods are really focused on particular places and venues, but some businesses and brands are also using Foursquare to drum up business another way: by offering brand badges.

Brand Badges

What do MTV, Starbucks, Zagat, Bravo, and the Pennsylvania Department of Tourism have in common? They are all promoting themselves through special badges. Offering special event or promotional badges is well beyond most businesses: They come with a multi, thousand-dollar price tag on them to start with. However, offering brand badges is something to keep on your radar. Foursquare could at some point open up badges from being exclusive to certain brands; it could also lower the price tag. I hope it does. Having a set of badges to go with a museum visit would be fun. Or a group of local businesses could get together and offer a "tour our town" badge that can be unlocked only by visiting enough of the participating stores.

It's an appealing idea to earn badges, buttons, pins, or stickers for doing things in the real world, so if venues can offer specials, it would be nice if they could offer badges, too.

Facebook Deals

If an area of social media is really starting to catch on, you know that the "big boys" will start getting interested, and in this case the biggest kids in the schoolyard are Google and Facebook. Are Google and Facebook interested in location check-in and how to attract businesses? You bet they are. In Lesson 10, "Competitors and What's Next," I'll go into more detail on how Google and Facebook are in the game, but for this lesson it's all business, and business is heating up.

Initially launching in the United States and moving into other countries over time, Facebook's Deals is very much like how Foursquare's deals work, except that Facebook is behind them. Facebook Deals falls into the "we saw this coming a mile away" category. Facebook is about connecting the dots between its members and businesses and making the connections meaningful. Meaningful ads or deals are based on your location, your social network, and where you've already checked in with Places. Deals is in the early stages of its rollout and there aren't examples galore to show off here.

Setting Up a Deal

The first step before you can make a deal is to claim your business on Facebook Places. As you can imagine, that's a little beyond the scope of this book; however, so as not to leave you completely in the lurch, here are the basic steps:

1. Find your business on Facebook Places by checking in with a mobile device (such as an iPhone). You might have to add your business on Places if no one has checked in there yet.

2. At Facebook.com, you'll need to search for your business and claim it as your own.

3. Like Foursquare, Facebook will confirm with you (a real person) that you are really the owner of the business.

4. After these details are worked out, you can start offering deals to your customers.

Facebook Deals (again, currently only in the United States) falls under several types:

- ▶ Individual (only when someone checks in)

- ▶ Group (when you check in with friends)

- ▶ Loyalty (after so many check-ins you get something; think loyalty cards without having to remember the card)

- ▶ Charity (a donation is given to a customer's charity of choice by you, the business, when the customer checks in)

Just as Foursquare offers, Facebook Deals is aimed at not only getting people to check in (which is a boon to Facebook), but to build customer loyalty for you and your business. And also like Foursquare, a key component with Deals is in redeeming offers and coupons.

Redeeming

Your Facebook Deals should be easy to redeem. They're usually the "show the cashier" kind of offer, and that is the key—make sure your staff members know all about the deal. There is nothing more frustrating to a customer to be offered a deal and then be unable to redeem it because the person at the register hasn't heard of it and won't accept it. This happens in the real world as well, and I'm sure it's happened to you in the past, so don't allow the same thing to happen to your customers with Foursquare offers, Facebook Deals, or Google Places coupons.

Google Places and Google Hotpot

One of the things that Foursquare is lacking is the capability to rate places (even Facebook Places doesn't have this). Now, building off the success of other location rating tools such as Yelp, Google has launched Hotpot. In itself, Google Hotpot doesn't have much to do with your business or offering deals; sure, people can rate your business with 1–5 stars, but that isn't about offering a deal or promotion. Google Hotpot, however, is tied into and powered by Google Places, and this is where you need to get involved. As a business, you can claim ownership of your Place in Google Places.

Google Places is what you get when you look up a business name or type a search term such as "dentist Vancouver" in Google and then you see the address and map in the result. I'll cover the high-level details of how you claim your business in Google Places. First, look for your business in Google. When it comes up in the result, click it and choose to claim it. Like Foursquare and Facebook, Google will want details such as your phone number, and it will contact people so it can verify that you are the owner. After that's done, you can start creating coupons.

Right now, Google coupons are only available in the United States and the coupons are intended (like those from Facebook Places and Foursquare) to be used on mobile devices. When someone looks up a business on Google Places, ostensibly to get information such as your hours, address, website, or phone number, they can also see that you have a coupon available. Here's how you create a coupon on Google Places:

1. Log into Places on Google.

2. Click the Coupons tab in the upper-left to create a coupon.

3. Fill out all the information for your coupon, preview it, and make sure you're happy with the way it looks.

4. Click Continue when you're done.

According to Google, your coupon should appear on the site in 24 hours. Be patient—refreshing over and over doesn't help!

Remember, like all coupon offers both real and virtual, make sure your staff knows about the offer, the rules, and the details.

Managing Location Services

At this point, you might be wondering how you're going to manage all these different accounts, offers, and location profiles. A new Vancouver-based startup named Geotoko (geotoko.com) saw this pain coming and has some help on the way.

Geotoko allows you to manage all your location services profiles (Foursquare, Gowalla, Yelp, Facebook Places, with more coming) in one place. Not only that, Geotoko manages your statistics, location claims, and, best of all, all the offers and coupons across your locations. Geotoko is a relatively new startup. However, as location services are becoming more popular, I suspect that Geotoko will have more than its share of customers in the future.

Summary

Foursquare is fun, interesting, and a good tool for finding new things to do when you're out and about. Businesses can use Foursquare in a number of ways to promote themselves to get more business. Loyalty rewards are nothing new to business owners, but Foursquare takes it to the next level, enabling a business to not only offer discounts, freebies, and special deals but also learn more about the people who are coming into the business. Foursquare users are a growing segment of the online population. If you get in on the Foursquare action early and give great deals, there's a good chance you might gain a loyal following from a connected part of society. The best part is that claiming your venue and offering specials is free (beyond the cost of the special to you), so there is no risk or harm in getting started.

It doesn't end with Foursquare either—don't forget Facebook and Google in your location-based coupon plans. Foursquare might have a head start, but Google and Facebook are huge players and are sure to influence, if not drive, the market in the near term.

LESSON 10

Foursquare's Competitors and What's Next

In this lesson you'll learn about some of Foursquare's main competitors and why you might like to try them, too. Not only that, you'll get a glimpse into what is coming down the road in the location awareness space.

Looking at Foursquare's Competitors

Foursquare isn't the only kid in town, as far as location awareness goes. It has several new (and old) competitors. Foursquare wasn't even the *first* game in town—that honor goes to Brightkite—but it's been capturing a lot of attention recently. Maybe it's the game aspect of it or the badges you can earn. In any case, Foursquare is capturing more and more attention of late. But a lot (and very little) changed overnight when the 300-pound-gorilla of social networking and social media got in on the game (so to speak): Facebook launched Places in August 2010. This lesson is about the other players in the location game and also takes a stab at what might be coming down the pike in the future.

When you create something interesting and catchy, other people copy it. Yes, imitation is the sincerest form of flattery, but when you're trying to build a business from it, it's another matter. Foursquare is no different, and they have several interesting competitors who all offer something a little different to the location game party.

Facebook Places

This book took, roughly, three or four months to publish. In the final stretch, something rather interesting happened: In August 2010, social networking juggernaut Facebook (www.facebook.com) announced its long-anticipated Places feature, which allows people to locate themselves and friends (see Figure 10.1). Starting the next day, people across the United States could start checking into Places on Facebook. As you can imagine, I watched the announcement with more than a bit of trepidation. Could, in a single hour, my months of hard work be flushed away? The immediate answer is "No."

Facebook invited representatives from Gowalla, Yelp, *and* Foursquare to attend its announcement, which was a signal to all of us that Facebook was going to try to *build on* the work of others instead of crushing them into oblivion. In fact, the day *after* the Facebook Places announcement, Foursquare saw its largest day ever for creating new accounts. Foursquare, Gowalla, and Yelp will be able to tap into the new Facebook Places API from within *their* applications. What this means and what it will look like is unclear right now; however, the good thing is that Facebook isn't trying to take over the location and check in scene, but work with it.

Like Foursquare, you check into places with Facebook Places. You can see from Figure 10.1 that you can choose from places that are close to where you are (the Facebook mobile application works just like the Foursquare application does). The interesting thing about Facebook is that when you check in you can "tag" other friends who are there with you. Your friends have to approve the tag and you can opt out of being tagged in the first place; however, you have to take that extra step to opt-out in your Facebook privacy settings.

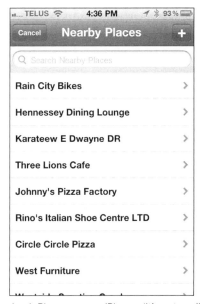

FIGURE 10.1 Facebook Places, on my iPhone. (It's not available in Canada yet.)

FIGURE 10.2 Checking in with Facebook Places and the tag your friends box is visible.

One of the interesting features of Places, and the one that is raising the most privacy alarm bells, is that your Facebook friends can tag you in Places as an interim step of checking in. Of all the new features in Facebook Places, this is the one that has the potential to be both the most fun and the most problematic. How it all plays out only time will tell.

> **NOTE**
>
> You can turn off friends tagging you in Places (it is on by default). In addition, you have to confirm that you want to check into a place on Places.

At this writing, it's still too early to tell how Foursquare will fit into Facebook Places. We know that Foursquare will be able to send users' information to and from Places, but beyond that, we don't know much. Facebook has, however, legitimized location awareness as something that people like and will continue doing and that can help companies make money. If nothing else, that's a pretty big win, I think.

Gowalla

Gowalla (www.gowalla.com) is very much like Foursquare, except it offers pins instead of badges (see Figure 10.3).

Gowalla is often considered a pretty upstart in the location game (see Figure 10.4). Gowalla's site was so pretty, in fact, that it prompted Foursquare to update its website (which now looks very much like Gowalla's).

Despite its good looks, Gowalla is still struggling to catch on. If Foursquare is considered to *just* be hitting the mainstream, Gowalla still has a bit to go. Will Places increase awareness of Gowalla, as it has for Foursquare? I'm not sure, but it probably will.

FIGURE 10.3 Earning a pin in Gowalla on my iPhone.

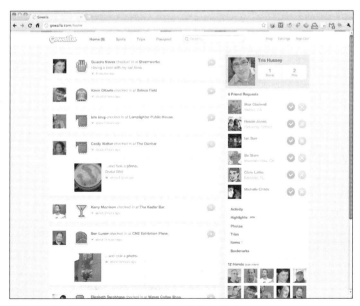

FIGURE 10.4 My profile page on Gowalla's website.

Brightkite

Brightkite (www.brightkite.com) was one the early contenders in the location awareness space, but it has lost its luster of late. It has all the basics but lacks the sizzle of Gowalla and Foursquare that makes location awareness a game and fun. If Brightkite can link up with Facebook Places, it will certainly have a good chance at picking up more users. Otherwise, Brightkite might remain a niche player in an already niche market.

Brightkite shows that even if you're first to market, you're not guaranteed success. When Foursquare was just an upstart, Brightkite had users and a full suite of apps for people to use; however, they failed to catch the imagination of users (and maybe fun) like Foursquare did.

Yelp

Yelp (www.yelp.com) didn't start out with much emphasis on location awareness; rather, it was about reviews of locations (see Figure 10.5). Sure, Yelp *knew* where you were, but only so it could recommend a good place near you for whatever it is that you were looking for.

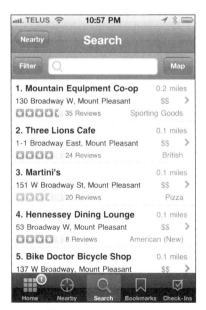

FIGURE 10.5   Yelp on an iPhone, showing locations and their star ratings.

Yelp's main claim to fame was that its users would visit places and rate them. Great ratings could bring lots of customers. Bad ratings...well, you can figure that out. In mid-2010, Yelp started to get into the checking in game as well (see Figure 10.6). As with Foursquare, with Yelp you can become a ruler of your location (it uses the terms *duke* and *duchess* instead of *mayor*).

Like Gowalla and Foursquare, Yelp is working with Facebook on Places. Now, in terms of being a *useful* addition to Places, Yelp has a good chance of helping people not only see where their friends are but whether they're hanging out at a good place. If they aren't, maybe you could direct them to a better choice (maybe where you are duke or duchess, so you can get a good perk).

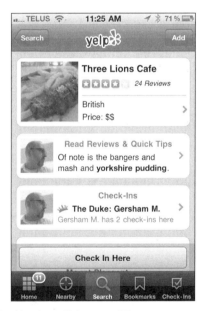

FIGURE 10.6 Checking in on Yelp on an iPhone.

Google Hotpot

One of Google's greatest strengths is its tremendous database of information. When we want to find something on the Internet, where do most of us go? That's right, Google. Google has even become a verb meaning to look something up on the Internet (of course, most of us also use Google for the looking as well). You've probably noticed that when you look up a type of business or a specific business, you often get a result that brings up a Google pagewith information about that business. This is Google Places (yes, it's a confusing name, I know), and now Google is letting you rate places (such as Yelp) using a service called Hotpot. Initially available only online and for Android phones, at the moment Google Hotpot is more of a threat to Yelp than to Foursquare. (Google has already been integrating a lot of Yelp's reviews into its results.)

Simply searching at www.google.com/hotpot/ allows you to find places close to you and see how people have rated businesses you are interested in. For example, if you are looking for sushi in Vancouver (Vancouver, by the way, has some of the best sushi in North America), you might get a result like that seen in Figure 10.7.

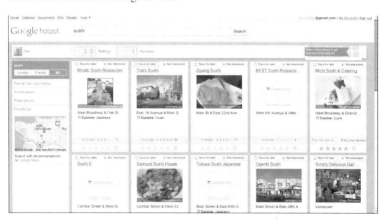

FIGURE 10.7   Searching for nearby sushi in Vancouver.

Although Google Hotpot is a new addition to the Google family of location services, the fact that Google has gotten into the location and ratings area means that, together with Facebook, Google is betting big on this emerging market. All these potential ways to check in and rate businesses brings up an important question—which service is right for you?

Picking the Right Service for You

Now that you're thoroughly confused about location services, you're probably wondering which one you should use. Yes, as you can gather, I have accounts on all of them. Call it an occupational hazard. There is a simple way to choose the service for you: Go where your friends are.

If your friends are talking about Foursquare or Gowalla or Yelp, that's the service for you. Sure, this book is about Foursquare, but any of these services has the potential to be more fun and interesting if that's where your *friends* are. Being the only person you know in your area on Foursquare isn't much fun at all. Now, if you're the vanguard of your group testing out new apps, well you know enough about Foursquare to give it a good shot. Then the next challenge is to get your friends using Foursquare.

Gowalla, as you can tell, is very, very similar to Foursquare, so I don't consider it an alternative per se. Yelp, however, offers something cool enough that I would suggest joining Yelp as well as Foursquare. No, I'm not setting up for my next book. The reason is that Yelp offers reviews of places in addition to the check in aspect. When you're looking for a great place to eat or go or shop, often Yelp has some of the best "regular folks" reviews around. Even if I don't *check in* using Yelp, I often check Yelp when I'm looking for honest reviews about something.

Then there are Facebook and Google's offerings, just to make things interesting (confusing?). So, like using Yelp and Foursquare together, I think Facebook Places and Google Hotpot are services that are complementary to all the others. Facebook Places is going to tie in with all the services discussed here (except for Google Hotpot), so that isn't going to be an either-or situation. Google Hotpot and Yelp? Right now, Hotpot doesn't have the user base or ratings to replace Yelp, so the two will complement each other for some time to come. No question, though: Location services are hot and getting hotter online.

Will there be ways to check into several services at once the way you can use an app like Tweetdeck to update your Twitter and Facebook account at the same time? Probably so, but they haven't come to the fore as yet. That said, I wouldn't be surprised if someone builds a Facebook app that uses Places to check you into all your services at once.

Are We Tired of Sharing Our Lives?

With all the social media available today, including so many location-based sites, are we sharing too much? It is indeed important to keep privacy and security in mind while you learn the ropes of Foursquare. I certainly ask myself a number of questions: "Do I want to check in here?" "Do I want people to know where I am?" "Do I know this person well enough to trust him or her with this information?"

As I was researching this book, I started creating profiles on a number of services. It's a rather annoying and tedious process—and, as a friend asked, "Do we really need another service?" Believe it or not, I think we do need a few different options for location-based services, and I think Facebook Places might wind up being a great boon for all of them. With Places, you can use a Yelp account to track ratings and use Foursquare to keep track of your friends' comings and goings. If things work as I *think* they will, you'll be able to have all this within Facebook Places.

Location is just another facet of our increasingly transparent lives. An important facet of this kind of transparency is knowing when (and how) to turn it off. I choose not to check into all the places I go (like a doctor's appointment or a friend's house) and sometimes I check in off the grid if I want to record that I was somewhere, but don't want to tell the world. I hope if you've learned one thing from this book it's when to go off the grid and be less transparent, instead of more. Remember if you want to check into a place, but keep that check in private either uncheck or tap "No" on "Share with friends" when you check in. Just because you *can* tell the world where you are, doesn't mean you *should*.

Until then, check in early and check in often.

Summary

Do you know where your friends are right now? Not long ago you might answer something like "at home or work, I guess" because we didn't really *know* where people were at any given time. Now with services like Foursquare, if you're heading out for a bite to eat or shopping you can see where your friends are and connect with them if you want. Welcome to the world of location awareness.

As a society, we're still working through how we are going to really tap into these new services. Right now, Foursquare and its ilk are mostly fun. In the future, however, I see the potential for being able to learn more about your surroundings. Things like, history, special offers from stores, traffic reports, events going on. Things that are tied to where you are at that moment in time. While this might seem rather creepy to many people (including me sometimes), the fact is that we will be able to benefit from knowing where our friends are and what they recommend doing in a certain place.

All you have to do is check in.

LESSON 11

Foursquare and Yelp

In this lesson, you'll learn how Foursquare and Yelp are complementary services to each other, and while they do overlap in some respect, there are several things you can get in one that you can't get in the other.

After finishing Lesson 10, I wouldn't be surprised if you felt a little confused. Having several options to do things *like* Foursquare but that aren't Foursquare is a little overwhelming. Not that competition is new to the online world; it's what has inspired those of us in the online startup world to keep trying, improving, and pushing to create the next big thing. Foursquare and Yelp (and Gowalla and Facebook Places) are just a couple of examples—MySpace and Facebook are similar social networking services; Hotmail, Gmail, and Yahoo Mail are web-based email providers; and Posterous, Tumblr, WordPress.com, and Blogger are just a few of the places you can start a free blog. So, what makes Foursquare and location-services/apps any different?

It doesn't, and that's why there is an entire lesson on competitors in this book. But competitors *can* complement each other, and here's how you can use Yelp and Foursquare together.

Complementary Competitors

If you remember from Lesson 10, Yelp didn't start off with check-ins (or dukes/mayors) at all—they added that feature later to better compete with what Foursquare was offering. The essential part of all services such as Yelp and Foursquare is a loyal user community. If people start using another app instead of yours for something, that is one step closer to people not using your app at all. Not good for a startup, not good at all. So, let's look at Yelp and Foursquare as tools you can use together.

If you look at what each service set out to do when it launched, you can see how each of these tools can be used together. Foursquare started as a way for friends to see where other friends were and to go hang out with them (as well as finding new places to hang out). Yelp, on the other hand, was all about giving businesses ratings on their service. Good restaurant or *great* restaurant? Great mechanic, boutique, cafe, store…you get the idea. Yelp let you browse, based on your current location, for what you were looking for based on ratings, price, distance, and whether it was even open (that's pretty helpful). If you're looking for tacos at 1 AM within a mile of where you are now, Yelp is the tool for you. Foursquare might be able to tell you what's close, but not what's good or what's open. On the other hand, if you are out on the town and looking to hang out where your friends are (or wherever the hot place of the night is), looking up your friends on Foursquare is your choice. And once you know *where* your friends are, you can go back to Yelp and find out if your friends are in a total dive or a swanky, hip place to be. Let's walk through the example of looking for a place for dinner and see how the two apps can work together.

Example: Finding a Romantic Restaurant

Let's say you're planning a romantic dinner. You want to make a good impression, but you also don't want to break the bank, either. You know the area of town you want to be in: maybe one with great places for coffee or dessert, or dancing and fun nearby. You know that some of your friends have good taste in restaurants, so you're asking around to get recommendations, but you're also Internet-savvy so you're not just stopping there— you're going to try Yelp for help.

NOTE

This example is based around having a Yelp account as well as a Foursquare account. If you don't have a Yelp account yet, head over to Yelp.com and set one up. The process is pretty much the same as for Foursquare.

The first step isn't going to be performed with the mobile client, but at the Yelp website. In the top search bar I searched for "romantic dinner" and because Yelp knows who and where I am, Vancouver was already filled in. The results were pretty encouraging: 40 restaurants around Vancouver (see Figure 11.1).

FIGURE 11.1 Initial search for "romantic dinner" in and around Vancouver.

This is a good start. I see a lot of reviews and some good information, but let's refine things a bit. Using the checkboxes (and clicking More below the criteria, as well), I can narrow it down to nine possible places, sorted by Highest Rated (see Figure 11.2).

FIGURE 11.2   Filtered results based on location, price, and other factors.

For the sake of this example, I'll go out on a limb and say that #3 looks good. Sure, The Teahouse is great (it is a very popular restaurant here in Vancouver), and Octopus Garden looks nice, but I think nothing says romance like French cuisine, so Bistrot Bistro it is! Let's look at the reviews (see Figure 11.3).

If you check the rating distribution graph near the bottom of the screen, you'll note that, by and large, the restaurant gets mostly four- and five-star reviews, with a few ones and twos. A few bad ratings for are unavoidable, so I think that's okay. I select Mid-price as one of my filters so I know the dinner might be a little pricey, but I know what I'm in for. The default sorting is for my friends to show up first. Because none of the people who've left a review happen to be friends of mine, I click the link to sort by Elites. Elites are people who have submitted a lot of reviews that have also been well received (read, *accurate*). From that sort, I see people who seem to give high-quality ratings and generally like the place. But what about my friends? This is where Foursquare is going to come in.

FIGURE 11.3 Reviews for Bistrot Bistro. Looks good, might be time to make a reservation.

Switching over to Foursquare.com, I search for "Bistrot Bistro" and see that, again, none of my friends have checked in there (they might have gone there, but just not checked in), but there is a nice review. I was thinking the chocolate mousse was going to be the dessert of choice, but based on the review, I might go for crepes now (see Figure 11.4).

Now I'm ready to make the reservation—and if I'm using either the Yelp or Foursquare mobile clients, I can call the restaurant with a quick tap or click. You can compare and contrast the interfaces for this in Figure 1.5 (for Yelp) and Figure 1.6 (for Foursquare).

FIGURE 11.4   None of my Foursquare friends have been there, either, but there is a tip from another Foursquare user.

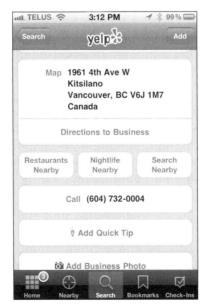

FIGURE 11.5   Venue information for Bistrot Bistro on Yelp for iPhone.

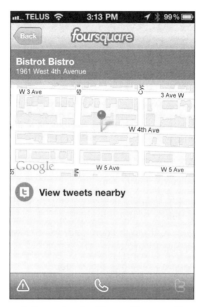

FIGURE 11.6   Venue information for Bistrot Bistro on Foursquare for iPhone.

Personally, I think the Yelp interface is much more helpful! Now, whether *I* check in depends on my dinner companion. However, when it's all said and done, I'll certainly make sure I submit my own review on Yelp and something on Foursquare. After all, if you're going to use these services, it's important that you contribute to them as well. It's what makes them work for everyone involved.

One other use for Foursquare when going to this place is to check to see who is already there that I might know. Just in case I do (or don't) want to say "hi" while we're there.

It's as simple as that—Foursquare wasn't built to help you find a romantic (or otherwise) place to have dinner; it was designed to help you connect with your friends while you're out. Yelp is designed to help you find a good place, and, although there is a check-in function now, that certainly isn't the main focus of Yelp (nor should it be).

Foursquare, Yelp, and Google Hotpot

Just because I'm like this, I'm going to muddy the waters a little bit. As I'm working on this book, the entire landscape of locations services is changing. Foursquare is still the king of the hill, but Yelp has new competition from Google with a similar ratings product called Hotpot.

Hotpot (named for a communal Chinese meal with boiling broth and goodies you and your friends cook together) takes the information already in Google's Places tool for finding businesses and adds a ratings component. Right now Google Hotpot is still new and doesn't have any check-in function, mayors or dukes, or filtering, like Yelp does. However, we have all seen what Google can do to the competition if it wants to bring the full power of its search empire to bear. Expect the feature set to evolve, possibly even by the time you're reading these pages.

Should Yelp be concerned? Most assuredly. Yelp is probably looking over its shoulder now, but maybe for a potential purchase by Google (that would be a smart move, I think) instead of just being stomped into oblivion. In the short term, Google Hotpot is so new that rankings for many businesses are incomplete (if they exist at all), so substituting Hotpot for Yelp in the previous example wouldn't work—the features just aren't there. In the longer term, who knows? What is becoming clear is that people do like to use tools to find their friends *and* to learn more about where they are going. Right now, I'd say you can't do much better than pairing Yelp and Foursquare.

Summary

You might think that services with overlapping functions could be mutually exclusive, but in the case of Foursquare and Yelp, you'd be missing out on using two really powerful tools. Yelp is a great tool if you want to find out what the best place for something is, and Foursquare is the tool to see whether anyone you know is there right now. Using the strengths of both services allows you to get more out of both of them. Try it and see for yourself.

LESSON 12

Foursquare and Gowalla

In this lesson, you'll learn that having accounts on Foursquare and Gowalla might not be such a bad thing after all. Although the two services compete for the same kind of features and attention, Gowalla is offering some interesting features that you might like to check out.

One of the interesting (read "frustrating and maddening") parts about writing a book on one of the hottest segments in social media, location services/games, is that the whole landscape is shifting and changing. Like the previous chapter on Yelp, this one on using Gowalla and Foursquare could have been written several different ways depending on when I sat down to write it. Right now, it's late 2010 and, shall we say, "the game is afoot" because Gowalla is doing some pretty interesting things to get attention and users in an attempt to carve out a new space in the market.

Same Goal, Different Stickers

At the most simplistic level, Gowalla is essentially like Foursquare, except you receive stickers and pins when you complete certain tasks or trips (see Figure 12.1). That, however, is the simplistic look at Gowalla. Gowalla helps map things like a trip you take (with check-ins along the way) and leave secret, private notes for friends when they check into a certain location. For example, building on the last lesson's use of Yelp to find a romantic restaurant, you could ask your beloved to marry you by leaving a special note for her that can only be unlocked when she checks in at the restaurant using Gowalla. Fine, I'm a geek and maybe only a geek would think of such a thing, but that's just one example. If you get a little creative, you'll soon find there are plenty of ways to put this service to use.

FIGURE 12.1   Gowalla separates itself from Foursquare by focusing on creative activities related to checking in at various locations.

Gowalla has been trying to be different from Foursquare since it launched. Initially Gowalla was Foursquare with a prettier website and app, but soon that charm wore off. What then? The "what then" became making Gowalla about activities *and* making it so people didn't have to choose between the two services.

More on not needing to choose in a moment, but let's talk about activities first.

Disney and More

Gowalla's focus is on the journey and the trip, not as much about where your friends are. It's more about *you* than *them*, so in the fall of 2010 Gowalla started creating more stamps for special locations. Taking a trip to Europe? There are special stamps for that. Are you an avid sports fan?

Well, if you check in at many college arenas, or at any NFL, NHL, or NBA stadium, there are stamps for all of them. Like Cirque du Soleil? There are stamps for all of those, as well. Maybe the best of all are Disneyland and Walt Disney World. Gowalla worked with Disney to create stickers not just for the parks, but also the attractions within the parks. Yes, you can get your Pirates of the Caribbean and Haunted Mansion stickers.

This gives a different twist to the whole "check in so you know where I'm hanging out" idea. Gowalla is working on "check in so you can map and remember where you've been." Okay, nice difference. Interesting, but is it enough to warrant creating accounts on *both* Gowalla and Foursquare, *and* having to check in with both apps all the time? Seriously? Even as a geek, I'm not too keen on saying "Oh wait, let me check in on Foursquare, Gowalla, Facebook Places, and…" not to mention my less geeky friends get rather tired of me stopping to check and tap and type and tap.

What if, after you set up accounts on both services, you could use one application to check in on all those places at once? Pretty interesting, pretty cool, and exactly what Gowalla did.

One App to Rule Them All

In what I think was a brilliant move, Gowalla is updating all its applications to allow you to not only check in on Gowalla, but Foursquare and Facebook as well (see Figure 12.2). Even more interesting is that you also see the check-ins from your friends on those services, too. So, while it once meant using Gowalla or Foursquare (or having to use them both at the same time), you can choose to use the Gowalla app, but still keep up with all your Foursquare activity as well. This update has given me a whole *new* reason to try Gowalla, because Gowalla isn't forcing me to make a choice at all. I get the best of both worlds.

FIGURE 12.2   Checking into my local Starbucks with Gowalla, but cross-checking into Facebook Places and Foursquare.

Another interesting thing about Gowalla is that unlike Foursquare, it has a dedicated iPad app. Sure, I can use the iPhone app on my iPad, but it appears in "iPhone size," whereas the Gowalla for iPad application takes full advantage of the larger screen and features of the iPad. Okay, maybe this isn't a *huge* thing, but it is certainly worth a side note for iPad fans like myself.

Gowalla's biggest challenge was that it essentially was fighting to get people to choose it over Foursquare. Sure, the apps each had a slightly different take on locations, but in reality, to most people it came down to one or the other. Even within my tech-geek, early-adopter crowd, folks tend to pick one service or tool to use for a given task: We're not big on overlap.

This is why a lot of services fade, are bought up, or have to define their own new niche to survive. Gowalla decided to attack this problem head on by not forcing a choice to be made. However, there is the matter of whether Foursquare or Gowalla is the service you want to spend time on?

Go Where Your Friends Are

Even though you *can* use Gowalla to check in on Foursquare, you're wondering why the heck would you want to sign up for yet another service that does something that Foursquare already does? Seriously? Another username and password to remember, more friends to find and manage, more emails to get—I completely agree with you. Beyond the fact that I *have* to sign up and try all these services because it's my job and what I do, with most services I sign up for, I don't ever return and use them. If the service doesn't solve a problem I'm having, why should I keep using it?

I keep using the services and applications (especially the social media ones) *if all my friends are using it, too*. Which is exactly my recommendation for you with Gowalla and Foursquare. Sure, this whole book has been about Foursquare, and Foursquare is still the leader of the pack in terms of number of users, number of check-ins, and venues, but maybe your close friends are all using Gowalla (or Yelp, although you know from Chapter 11 that Yelp and Foursquare are very complementary to each other). If that's the case, maybe you sign up for both but spend most of your time in Gowalla. Or you sign up for both services and use Foursquare because all your friends are there, or the places you frequent are offering better deals for Foursquare users. The bottom line is that you use the service that works best for you. All the services are in competition for your attention. They are all going to be offering better and better applications, and encouraging businesses to offer better and better deals to customers.

Summary

Not long ago, my advice would simply have been to choose whichever
service most appeals to you and that's used by the largest number of your
friends. However, Gowalla's recent moves toward working more closely
with competitors and offering new ways to map out your travels makes
me think the choice might just come down to which app you simply like
more. Sure, if you check in with Foursquare using Gowalla, you might
need to wander to the Foursquare app now and then to check on deals and
badges, but day-to-day you might just like the look, feel, and features of
Gowalla better. And if you're an iPad user, you'll certainly appreciate
using an application that takes full advantage of what the iPad has to
offer. In the end, it's all up to you: what service your friends are using,
where the better offers and deals are centered, and which app you like
more.

Index

Sams**TeachYourself**

from Sams Publishing

Sams Teach Yourself in 10 Minutes
offers straightforward, practical answers
for fast results.

These small books of 250 pages or less
offer tips that point out shortcuts and
solutions, cautions that help you avoid
common pitfalls, notes that explain
additional concepts, and provide additional
information. By working through the
10-minute lessons, you learn everything
you need to know quickly and easily!

When you only have time for the answers,
Sams Teach Yourself books are your
best solution.

Visit **informit.com/samsteachyourself**
for a complete listing of the products
available.

FREE Online Edition

Your purchase of **Sams Teach Yourself Foursquare in 10 Minutes** includes access to a free online edition for 45 days through the Safari Books Online subscription service. Nearly every Sams book is available online through Safari Books Online, along with more than 5,000 other technical books and videos from publishers such as Addison-Wesley Professional, Cisco Press, Exam Cram, IBM Press, O'Reilly, Prentice Hall, and Que.

SAFARI BOOKS ONLINE allows you to search for a specific answer, cut and paste code, download chapters, and stay current with emerging technologies.

Activate your FREE Online Edition at www.informit.com/safarifree

> **STEP 1:** Enter the coupon code: QDLTREH.

> **STEP 2:** New Safari users, complete the brief registration form. Safari subscribers, just log in.

If you have difficulty registering on Safari or accessing the online edition, please e-mail customer-service@safaribooksonline.com